Praise for Th

"In a world where most of us are successful at everything except life, *The Spark* is a must read. It will jump-start your life!"
- Jacob Israel Liberman, vision scientist author of *Luminous Life: How the Science of Life Unlocks the Art of Living*

"Stephanie James puts life in perspective. She simplifies what we all perceive as complicated. You want happiness? You want fulfillment in your life? Quit over complicating things, read her book and put a spark back in your life."
-Weldon Long, Author *The Upside of Fear, Consistency Selling & The Power of Consistency* A NYT & WSJ Bestseller

"A compelling and inspiring book! Stephanie James has drawn on her skills and experience as a psychotherapist as well as her own journey into "self and spirit" transforming her life, as she writes. *The Spark* is both a practical, down-to-earth guide to taking that journey ourselves and also a book that opens us to possibilities that we never imagined. Every page is filled with wisdom!"
-Elena Mannes, multi-award-wining independent documentary director/writer/producer and author *Soul Dog* and *The Power of Music: Pioneering Discoveries in the New Science of Song.*

"In *The Spark*, Stephanie James does a good job of compiling some of the most interesting and provocative material from her radio show. If you don't have time to listen to her show, you can find the wisdom here, all within one volume. James has identified valued threads from her interviews and other resources and tied them together here to provide inspiration for the reader".
- Stan Tatkin, PsyD, MFT psychologist and author of *We Do,* and *Wired for Love*

Praise for The Spark (continued)

"The Spark is an excellent guide. Step by step, psychotherapist Stephanie James shows how to gently examine beliefs that don't serve us, ways to develop more authentic and rewarding relationships (including with ourselves), and how to approach each day with zest. In a warm, conversational tone, James weaves together her 30 years of work with therapy clients, the latest research, and her own personal experience to create a wise and useful guide to finding your essence--and living it to the fullest."
-Marian Sandmaier, author, *Original Kin: The Search for Connection Among Adult Sisters and Brothers* and Features Editor for the *Psychotherapy Networker* magazine.

"In *The Spark: Igniting Your Best Life*, psychotherapist, author and coach Stephanie James reveals how our subconscious "inner life" can impact our all-too-conscious outer life. With kindness, clarity and plainspoken wit, she calls forth the spark in each of us that ignites our most extraordinary life. Whether you've been "working on yourself" for years or think that self-help is something you do on the buffet line, I guarantee this book has some inspiring and practical gems for you".
-Steve Bhaerman, comedian, radio host and co-author with Bruce Lipton, *Spontaneous Evolution*

Praise for The Spark with Stephanie James – Radio Show and Podcast

"Stephanie James has a marvelous gift. She is not only a natural interviewer, but her wisdom, poise, and grasp of key issues related to the human condition and the challenges we face are exceptional. I finished our interview feeling understood and heard, with a lingering sense of joy and satisfaction."
-Larry Dossey, MD, author of *ONE MIND: How Our Individual Mind Is Part of a Greater Consciousness and Why It Matters*

"Stephanie James is such a pleasure to listen to and learn from. Smart, good-hearted, funny, and wise!"
-Dr. Rick Hanson, New York Times bestselling author of Resilient: How to Grow and Unshakable Core of Calm, Strength, and Happiness

"My interview with Stephanie James was one of my favorites because Stephanie lives in her heart, making it easy to open up and share deeply."
-Jacob Israel Liberman, author of *Luminous Life: How The Science Of Light Unlocks The Art Of Living*

"Stephanie James is a master of creating interesting and dynamic interviews. She is blessed with a natural gift of getting beyond just the facts. She is the *next big thing* in the world of podcasts. Bottom line: her interview is the best I've experienced."
-Weldon Long, New York Times bestselling author of *The Power of Consistency*, and Consistency Selling

"Stephanie is profoundly genuine and I felt blessed to be seen and witnessed by her. And she has a wonderful way of gathering together some of the most forward-thinking minds of our time. Stephanie is a spark of hope for the world."
-Misa Hopkins, bestselling author of *The Root of All Healing* and the *Sacred Feminine Awakening* series

Praise for The Spark with Stephanie James –

Radio Show and Podcast
(continued)

"Perhaps the most enjoyable, playful, and thought-provoking time I've had in my years of having questions thrown my way. She uses her talents to ask important questions and she does so in a way that makes the experience fun for everyone."
-Mark S. Benn, Psy.D., author of *Stories from the Couch and Other Telling Tales*

"Stephanie James is a fabulous interviewer. She's bright, engaging, and thoughtful. I'm a Stephanie James fan."
-Dr. Stan Tatkin, Psy.D, Assistant Clinical Professor, Dept. of Family Medicine, UCLA

To hear these and other interviews from luminaries in the fields

of psychology, science, spirituality, business, and health

join us at:

www.thesparkpod.com

ISBN: 9781088570951
Library of Congress Control #002116612
Ignite Your Best Life Publications

The Spark
Igniting Your Best Life

Stephanie James

Dedication

For my daughters Acacia and Hailey.

You both came into world shining from the moment you were born.

I knew then, each one of you held an internal spark

that would help to light up and change the world;

I know you've definitely illuminated mine.

Shine on.

The Spark

Igniting Your Best Life

Stephanie James

Table of Contents:

Introduction

Over the last 30 years, it's been my greatest privilege as a counselor and psychotherapist to witness change and transformation in the individuals and couples I work with. I have spent long hours in deep connection with others as together we explored the content of their minds and the interiors of their hearts.

In my work with hundreds of individuals, it's become evident that there are some universal things we're all seeking: We're all seeking love. We're all seeking connection. And we're all seeking to make meaning of this often messy and unpredictable thing we call life.

We all want to live a life that feels rich, charged, and vibrant. It's not just enough for us to live a day-to-day, humdrum life. We want the sparks. We want to be lit up from the inside. We want to transcend the ordinary and live our best life in whatever way we define it. In order to live that best life, we often have to let go of old ways of thinking and being that keep us from living the kind of spark-filled life we truly desire.

Change is possible. Breaking through old thought patterns that no longer serve us is possible. Actualizing dreams and goals and creating a vibrant, balanced, and beautiful life—

it's all possible. I have seen the changes in my own life and I see the evidence in my office daily. So now, here we are together. It's your turn.

I've worked with individuals from CEOs to department chairs, from surgeons to students, as well as soldiers, lawyers, housewives, railroad workers, and all walks of life in between. My vision for this book is to share my almost 30 years of experience working with people as a mental health specialist, and my 50 years of life experience existing in this amazing, miraculous—and at times challenging—world. My hope is to help you see a clearer path for yourself, find a way to dig in and make change happen, and use specific proven techniques that have already helped thousands of people create richer, more fulfilling, and expanded lives. I trust that you will find your own golden nuggets within that will help elevate you to the next level of living your life as the best version of yourself. I am deeply grateful to have this opportunity to connect with you through this book and share this moment in your life.

In the last year, I've been the host of an inspiring, motivational radio show and podcast, *The Spark with Stephanie James*, which was designed to help others ignite their best lives. During that time, I've interviewed thought leaders and luminaires in such fields as psychology, spirituality, science, self-help, entrepreneurship and more. Guests on my show have included Bruce Lipton, Rick Hanson, David Burns, Stan Tatkin, Harriet Lerner, Weldon Long, Larry Dossey, Curt Richardson, Dan Siegel, Jacob Liberman, and Stephan A. Schwartz, to name a few. I've learned so much from their collective wisdom and experience, and I look forward to sharing their gifts and messages with you.

Personal note:

January 7, 2018

You know those mornings when everything seems to just line up, right? Those are the times when my brother would jokingly say, "I guess your rocks or stars or whatever are lined up—'cause things are goin' GOOD!" That's how my morning started on a beautiful pier at Benny's in Lake Worth, Florida. Everyone I encountered was friendly and authentically exuding a true glow of happiness. People were tremendously helpful, warm, and interactive, in a way that reminded me of my own beautiful and friendly hometown of Fort Collins, Colorado. My heart was full as I sat down to write the first words of this book. And then, my daily inspiration appeared on my phone. The title was "Trusting the Process" with a quote from Chantelle Renee:

"Aspects of ourselves die as we spiritually evolve. When we release what no longer serves our highest good, it is creating space for something better. This can be a painful process, but it is temporary. Don't hold on to the old, invite the new. What we resist will persist. Hold the vision and trust the process."

As I finished reading this, I again became aware of my surroundings, and Bob Marley's song that was playing at the café floated into my awareness. "This is my message to you…don't worry, about a thing… 'cause every little thing gonna be alright." This was my sign. The time was right to begin my book. Rocks and stars all lined up, brother.

I want to thank you for showing up too. I look forward to our journey together.

Chapter 1

The Beginning

"Every great dream begins with a dreamer.
Always remember, you have within you the strength, the
patience, and the passion to reach for the stars to change the
world."

—Harriet Tubman

spark \spärk\: anything that activates or stimulates;
inspiration or catalyst.

What does it mean to live a spark-filled life? It means
waking up to a morning full of possibility and potential that
you intentionally plug into. It means moving past your past
and leaning in fully to the present moment to create the
kind of future you want, full of joy, abundance, and
magical moments.

When you live a spark-filled life, you let go of old, limiting
beliefs and adopt new ones that ignite your spirit and heal
your heart. It's focusing on what you want to create in your
life and then taking the action to make it happen. There's

an amazing life that's available to you right now. You hold the flame within you to ignite your best life.

Have you ever spent any time around a newborn baby? Besides the occasional cry or whimper to be fed or changed, a newborn baby is living in bliss. This is pure essence at its finest. No worries, no judgments, no appointments to be late for, no places to rush to. It's just pure being-ness. It's ironic, then, that most people spend a good portion of their adult life trying to return to this state. Somewhere along the way, we forget who we are, and we become more like human "doings" than human "beings."

Babies have no need to compare themselves to each other. They don't think, "Hey, you've got designer diapers on and I don't!" They don't label themselves in any way: "Well, I'm more of an introverted baby, see, and I'm not very good at walking yet, and it's causing me some social anxiety." These are *not* the conversations that babies are having. Why not?

1. OK, the obvious. Babies don't have developed language centers in their brains yet.

2. They exist in present time, with no fear of the future or regrets from the past. They're truly just living in the moment. Pure beingness.

So much of my work has been to help people remember how to be in touch with this essence that's always fully alive within them at all times. It just often gets covered up with layers of life and needs further excavating to be accessed. It's always there, just waiting.

People are often brought to tears in my office when they are reminded of their true essence. They've focused on defining themselves through the roles they play, their career, their choices, as well as circumstances out of their control. Often, they've adopted a label that someone else put on them—"not smart enough," "not good enough," "not talented enough," "lazy," "black sheep of the family," "rebel," or "trouble maker"—and that becomes the lens that they continue to view themselves through in the world. It's my job to help them clear off that lens and to see their true selves more accurately.

The truth is that no one comes out of childhood unscathed. No matter how wonderful your childhood was or how amazing your parents were, somewhere along the way, you received less than rave reviews about yourself from someone in a position of importance. It may have been a coach, a teacher, or a Sunday school pastor. It may have been a crabby piano teacher, or a next-door neighbor, or even a doctor. When we were young, we were vulnerable and much more susceptible to being influenced by another person's image of us. Bruce Lipton says we are in a Theta brainwave state from birth to 7 and so we are absolutely impressionable to whatever messages we receive about ourselves and the relationships, circumstances and events happening around us and that these things begin to program our belief system and our subconscious mind. As children, we believed that adults somehow knew "the truth" about us because they were grown-up and because they were the "big people" we had the illusion that they had all the answers.

Now, here's where some of the trouble can start. It's like we have a filing cabinet in our minds. It stores the events in our lives and the messages we've received. It tends to purge the files that it doesn't think we need for survival, and it holds on to the thoughts, experiences, and beliefs it thinks we need to be safe. While this can be helpful—for example, touching a hot stove when you're five, the brain records that promptly: "Note to self: Do not touch hot stoves!"—there are other times when it's not helpful at all.

Negative experiences are like Velcro in the brain. Our brain holds on to them as a way to protect us and warn us if it seems as though they may happen again. Positive experiences are like Teflon. They slide right through. Our positive experiences aren't as easily retained because they aren't necessary for our survival. In order to get positive thoughts and experiences to "stick," repetition (repeating the positive thoughts or journaling about positive experiences) is the key to training your brain that these thoughts and experiences are important to hold on to.

You see, not everything in the belief files are true. Often, it's the messages we received during a painful moment that become the subconscious thoughts—that become our beliefs about ourselves. Like when we blew it on the football field and our coach yelled at us, or we tripped going up to give our speech in front of the class for student council, or the time we didn't wear the right clothes to school on the first day of fourth grade and the kids made fun of us. Embarrassing, humiliating, traumatic moments are the fodder for this file.

Begin Noticing

In order to uncover what these subconscious beliefs may be, it's important to start noticing what the messages are that you give to yourself daily. Are there negative or critical statements you catch yourself saying to yourself repeatedly? "I'm so stupid! I can't believe I did that again!" or "I'm such a klutz!" are examples of this. If you become aware of any of these negative patterns, congratulations! Awareness is the first step to healing them. When you identify these negative messages, it's time to take action.

One helpful exercise is to write them down and begin to gently dig into where those thoughts might have come from. Remembering the source and/or the absurdity of the situation in which they occurred can help us see the invalidity of these beliefs.

I remember hearing a story about a woman who was traveling with her brother (both adults in their 50s). She was very distraught because her second marriage was falling apart, and she was feeling very helpless to change anything about it. When her brother asked her what she thought had happened, she replied, "Obviously, I am not lovable! My first husband had an affair on me, and now this husband only spends time with his newly widowed 28-year-old daughter. They spend time snuggling on the couch and having intimate phone calls, and I am all by myself." Her brother then asked her where she got the idea, she was unlovable. "From Dad, of course!" She replied exasperated.

"He never hugged me, or held me on his lap, or told me that he loved me. Obviously, if my own father couldn't show me he loved me, I must not be lovable!"

Now, here's where the story gets interesting. Her brother then said to her, "It's so fascinating that you feel that way, because I remember night after night for months, Dad building you that doll house he gave you for Christmas when you were nine years old. Dad loved you. He just didn't know how to show you in the way that you needed it."

The story has a wonderful ending. As the sister took this newly learned information and assimilated it into her belief system, she was able to see that she'd taken her father's behavior and lack of demonstrativeness and interpreted it into a belief that she was unlovable. By gaining a new perspective of an old "untruth," she was able to see herself as being truly lovable, go home to her husband, and begin to experience herself and her relationship in new ways. Her marriage was saved, and she went on to have a much happier and fulfilling life.

Changing Your Beliefs

Once you begin to understand the roots of your negative beliefs, write out what you'd *like* to believe about yourself instead—even if you don't believe that new thought yet. The wonderful thing about your brain is that you actually have the power to condition and mold your file cabinet to work for you in a positive way. You can change what your brain notices, what it focuses on, and what kind of evidence it collects. It's actually quite simple. It just takes practice and consistency.

A powerful and proven way to improve your positive self-beliefs and your life is starting a 30-day belief journal. In this practice, you focus on one new positive belief you'd like to integrate into your belief system. Don't let the 30 days inhibit you. You only need to commit to a week at a time. Even after a week of doing this exercise, you'll start to notice the results, and this will only take you about five minutes a day, tops. Very little effort is required. But for the best results, follow through for 30 days to alert the brain that this is important business—and to make it stick. According to research, it takes about 25 to 30 days before a new habit, such as a new exercise routine or a healthier diet, becomes automatic. The same is true for developing new thoughts and beliefs.

At the top of the first page of your belief journal, write one new thought that you want to believe about yourself. (Remember, you don't have to believe it yet. Just write down what you *want* to believe.) At the end of each day, briefly write down of all the evidence that showed up that day to supports the new thought being true.

For example, when I was newly divorced and feeling very alone in the bigger world, my negative thought was "I have to do everything on my own." After taking an online course that discussed this 30-day journaling exercise and how it worked, I was anxious to put it to the test before I taught it to my clients. One of the ideas the course suggested was to make a new belief affirmation so big that when the positive evidence showed up, the mind couldn't refute it. I thought long and hard about what I wanted to believe, and then I wrote in my journal, "The universe completely loves and supports me!" Every day I wrote down the evidence that showed up during the day that supported my new desired belief.

What I began to discover was truly amazing. It started with noticing sweet little texts I'd receive from my team of girlfriends, such as "Love you sweet friend!" "Thinking of you!" Then I began to notice little events like being let into traffic and how kind people were to me at the grocery store and local café.

Two weeks after beginning the journal, I walked into the Starbucks I frequented on my way to work, and the barista said, "Stephanie, you always light up the place when you come in! This one's on me!" My beliefs about feeling loved and supported by the universe were really starting to take hold.

The following week, the lid was blown off my old belief system, never to return. I'd just bought my first home on my own, and I'd put most of my savings into fixing it up and making it livable for my daughter and me. As fate would have it, one weekend we'd gone up to Estes Park for the majority of the day, only to return to an inch of standing water in the basement where the old water heater had rusted out at the bottom. I felt overwhelmed and didn't know what to do. I went outside and in a very short amount of time, I had neighbors asking me what had happened and how they could help. They brought over fans and Shop- Vacs, and they helped me soak up the water and dry up the basement.

And as if that wasn't enough proof that I was loved and supported, there was a knock on my door shortly after we'd begun the cleanup process. One of my girlfriends and her husband lived four doors down and had seen all of the commotion. After I told her what had happened, she disappeared and returned 15 minutes later with a thousand-dollar check in her hand. "I know you don't have the money for this right now, but you need hot water for you and your daughter in the morning. My husband has a truck. You two can go pick up a water heater, and you can pay us back when you have the money." I was blown away. I *was* completely loved and supported by the universe! And it was showing up for me in a big way.

What was also amazing about this process is that this love and support showed up for me in other, more subtle ways as well. My mom and I became closer and began connecting daily on the phone. I became closer to my girlfriends. For 16 years, I'd been the person my family or friends reached out to for support, but I wasn't good at asking for help.

The role I'd continually played in my life, up until that point, was that of the caretaker. I was the therapist. The helper. I wasn't the one being helped. So, this was very foreign territory for me. During this time, one of my dear friends said to me, "Thank you so much for reaching out and being human! You've always been there for me, and it means so much to me and makes me feel so good to be able to finally be there for you!" The love and support had always been there for me. My brain just hadn't been tuned in to it.

It's a principle of physics: what we focus on will expand. There's a particular part of our brain called the reticular activating system (RAS), which is the gateway for information that comes into our brain. It's responsible for what the brain pays attention to and what it ignores. An example of how it works is when my 29-year-old daughter was pregnant for the first time. She would say, "Mom! Everyone is pregnant!! We are everywhere!" Of course, everyone was not pregnant. Her RAS had just honed in on what she was experiencing, so this is what she was noticing whenever a pregnant woman was around. The same thing happens when you buy a new car. Pretty soon you start seeing your car everywhere. Did they just have a sales run on cars just like yours? Nope. It's your RAS in action, tuned in to what you're focusing on now.

You can also start focusing on the positive experiences that are already happening in your daily life and you'll begin to notice a positive result. Focus on the good experiences as they are happening, and allow yourself to pause a moment and really take it in. Feel the good feelings associated with it, and as you marinate a moment on these feelings, your brain will attune to these experiences and you will begin to notice them showing up more and more in your life.

It's as if you're creating a blueprint or a template in your brain that says, "I experience good things." Eventually, your brain will automatically begin noticing more things that make you feel good. Even on "bad" days, noticing when someone smiles at you or is genuinely kind to you in any way will start to make you feel better.

I had the privilege of interviewing psychologist and *New York Times* best-selling author Rick Hanson on my radio show, and we discussed his latest book, *Resilient: How to Grow an Unshakable Core of Calm, Strength, and Happiness*. Rick is someone whose work I've read and deeply respected for a long time, so getting to interview him was like a 19-year-old getting to meet her favorite rock star. Our interview was a deep and meaningful experience for me. Rick embodies the essence of presence and of "loving kindness" from the Buddhist tradition. His kindness, compassion, and loving heart were apparent from the moment we started speaking.

During that interview, he shared his experience of having grown up in what he described as "a kind of C- childhood." Because he had an early birthday, and extremely bright, he'd skipped a grade. So, he found himself on a college campus at age 16, feeling out of place and awkward. Rick described himself as having low self-worth and being socially awkward.

What he intuitively began to do to change his self-concept was a powerful practice that ended up transforming his life and his experiences. Rick began to notice and take inventory of the little things in his everyday experiences that felt good. If someone said hi to him on campus, he would take it in and allow himself to bask in it (what he calls "marinating in it") for a few moments. He would register every kindness he encountered by focusing on it for a few deep breaths, which allowed his brain to really absorb and record it as something meaningful.

Pretty soon, he started noticing more and more people being friendly and kind to him. One day, some guys on campus stopped and asked him if he wanted to throw a football with them. Rick was thrilled. As he continued to collect these positive experiences internally, Rick started to grow a sense of belonging. His self-concept grew and improved substantially. He was able to change his life experience by focusing on what felt good.

We all have the power to do this. No matter what your life script has been, you can begin to start examining your thoughts, change the ones that limit you, and adopt new beliefs. From this new mindset, you can cultivate the positive feelings and right action that will lead you into a more positive future than you ever may have thought was possible.

Uncovering negative or limiting beliefs and rescripting them into more accurate ones is one of the most healing things you can do for yourself. It's like taking off an old, clouded lens off of your camera and replacing it with a brand new one through which you can see the world more clearly and yourself more accurately.

Healing Our Beliefs

Dr. Francine Shapiro is an American psychologist who originated and developed EMDR (Eye Movement

Desensitization and Reprocessing), a form of psychotherapy for resolving the symptoms of traumatic and other disturbing life experiences. With over 30 years of empirical research behind it, EMDR is a protocol utilized by the FBI with their agents who have experienced trauma and is also the protocol recommended by the military for soldiers experiencing Post- Traumatic Stress Disorder (PTSD). In addition, it's used internationally with children and adults who have experienced trauma in its various forms.

I've been an advanced-level EMDR practitioner for over a decade. Witnessing the way the brain can rewire itself and disentangle from trauma is nothing short of a miracle. EMDR is a remarkable treatment method used to heal the symptoms of trauma, as well as other emotional conditions. Extensive scientific research studies have shown that EMDR is the most effective and the most rapid method for healing PTSD (Post Traumatic Stress Disorder).

During highly emotional or traumatic incidents, negative beliefs such as, "I am not safe in this world," "I can't trust anyone," or "I will never be good enough," are hardwired into our brains. They become subconscious beliefs we have about ourselves. After the incident, our brains begin to scan the environment for evidence to prove what it already has filed as "the truth."

What many people don't realize is that trauma in the brain doesn't have to be what we call "big-*T* trauma," such as a car accident, a devastating divorce, or a natural disaster. Often, it's the "little-*t* traumas," such as being bullied or being painfully embarrassed as a child, that create a trauma response in the brain along with hardwired negative beliefs about ourselves.

My introduction to EMDR happened during a conversation with my father (who has also been a licensed psychotherapist for over 30 years). I'd asked him what the longest time was he'd had a client in therapy. He told me he'd done eight years of talk therapy with a soldier who had been in the Blackhawk Down incident, and who suffered from severe PTSD. This client had such severe anxiety that he was unable to work, go to restaurants or movies, or be around crowds. His client's life was basically confined to living in a small apartment, going to therapy, and having very limited social interaction.

After seeing this man for eight years, my father got trained and certified as an EMDR therapist, and he began using the EMDR protocol. In 12 weeks, this man was no longer my father's client. He'd rewired his brain, hugely reduced his trauma response, and was able to plug back into the world. But to me, the biggest testament to the power of this form of treatment was that a year later, my father was the officiant at this man's wedding in Cancun. The client had gotten his entire life back and was living it fully alive and without a trace of PTSD.

When I heard this story, I knew that I had to get my EMDR certification so that I could start helping people heal at a whole new level.

EMDR in My Own Life

Not only do I use EMDR with my clients, but I have used it for healing my own trauma. Francine Shapiro says that most of us have 10 to 20 negative events in our lifetimes that need to be reprocessed in order to let go of the negative beliefs created by them.

I'll use a very traumatic event I experienced as a teenager to show how EMDR works. When I was 19 years old, friends and I used to love to drive to Boulder to go to a dance club called Pogo's. After 10 p.m., the bar would let in under-21-year old customers, who were allowed to dance but not drink. We all had to wear wristbands so that we wouldn't be served alcohol. The problem was, we all drank before we were admitted to the club. With friends who were over 21, getting hard liquor ahead of time wasn't an issue.

On January 2, 1986, after a night of drinking and dancing at the club, I was riding home with a group of friends at 2 a.m. on a back road between Boulder and Longmont. As was common when we went out, the least drunk person drove home. That night, I'd drunk too much to drive, so I was a passenger in the car. It had snowed a couple of days earlier and the snow that had melted on the road during the day had turned into black ice. The combination of the alcohol in our driver's body, the curve in the road, and the black ice, all came together in one terrifying moment. Our car slid off the road sideways, hit the soft dirt on the side of the road, and began flipping over—one, two, three times— until we landed upside down in the middle of a farmer's field.

It all happened in slow motion. I remember vividly the first time the roof of the car hit the ground. Watching the world spin around me, I thought, "We're going to hit again." And we did. When we finally came to a stop, someone said, "I smell gas!" We tried to open the doors, but we couldn't. I had on boots with hard heels, so I kicked out the side window and helped get some of the people out. I heard other windows shattering as well. Soon, all six of us were out safely. Three of us, including me, were badly hurt and needed medical attention. Because it was so late at night, it took an hour and a half before we could flag anyone down to help us.

All of us survived. None of the three of us who were taken to the hospital that night were seriously hurt. We had a lot of stitches, bumps, and bruises between us, but no broken bones and no hospital stays. A miracle indeed.

After resting in bed for the next few days, I literally got up, packed my bags, and headed to the airport because I already had a plane ticket and a plan to go visit my friends from art school in Los Angeles. As the plane took off, I became extremely and painfully aware that I wasn't in control of the vehicle I was sitting in. My thoughts started spinning, and my breathing started coming hard and fast. I began to panic and weep. It was internal hell during the whole flight.

This is what PTSD looks like. For the next several years, I was unable to fly without crying. I would hold hands with the stranger beside me or drink enough liquor to numb myself out so that I could fly without terror. When someone else was driving the car I was riding in, I would experience extreme anxiety and an overwhelming feeling of being out of control. Finally, after a long time of avoiding flying at all costs, I went through EMDR so that I could attend my stepsister's wedding in Dallas. I had a limited break in my schedule, and it was unreasonable to drive the 24 hours there and back in three days.

Within four sessions, my anxiety around flying or having someone else drive was significantly reduced. After 10 sessions, I was able to fly without any anxiety and I've been flying the friendly skies and enjoying the ride ever since. I feel relaxed and in control of myself now, no matter who is driving. EMDR changed my life and my personal experience greatly.

Making the Subconscious Conscious

Whenever I use EMDR with clients, I introduce them to the way EMDR works by having them chose an event that they would rate as a 4 on a scale of 0 to 10 when they think of the traumatic event (0 being no disturbance; 10 being the greatest disturbance they could imagine). I find this is a helpful way to acclimate their brain to the process. Because they're able to experience the positive results from the first treatment, their brain feels safe dealing with even more traumatic issues.

One client's first EMDR (scale 4) session was about her habits of not being able to look down the darkened stairs to her basement at night and of jumping into bed to avoid anything "grabbing" her. At 48 years old, she said she'd had the behavior since she was a teenager. She realized it was a result of anxiety associated with the dark, but she really wasn't aware of what it had stemmed from.

By doing a technique called "floating back," I had my client close her eyes and imagine the current behavior and then see herself getting younger and younger until she was able to see where the anxiety had originated. When she was finally able to access it in her memory, she became aware that the fear had actually begun in junior high school after she'd seen the horror movie *Carrie*. There was a scene at the end of the movie in which someone was putting flowers on a grave and a hand shot up from the grave to grab the person.

Because it was the first horror movie my client had ever seen, it had actually traumatized her system in a way that caused her brain to believe "Be careful of the dark because things can jump out and grab you!" Although this was a subconscious belief, her behavior was still being controlled by it over 35 years later.

When my client came back a week after the first session of EMDR, she reported a significant improvement. She said she was aware of the darkened stairwell but felt she was walking by it with more ease. And she was able to just step into her bed at night, instead of jumping into it from a couple of feet away.

A week after her second EMDR session, she reported her anxiety was at a zero. During the previous week, she'd casually walked by the staircase at night and gotten into bed without even a thought as to what might be under it. She stated that it was often after she was in bed that she realized how completely relaxed she was, with no fear at all of darkened staircases or what was under her bed. Over a year later, she hadn't experienced a problem in that area again.

We have the power to change our beliefs. We can do the work ourselves and if needed, we can seek help from an expert to get rid of old beliefs that continue to affect us in negative ways. One of the ways to determine if a thought or belief might require EMDR is to notice if you've analyzed, intellectualized, and processed a past situation but you're still being triggered by it. If your reaction is stronger that a current situation warrants, there may be a subconscious belief that's caught in the "fight or flight" part of your brain. Rationalization and logic aren't going to rewire it for you. EMDR may be just the thing to help you change it so you can live your best life.

Spark Up Your Life: Chapter One- Top 5 Takeaways

1. The first step in creating a spark-filled life is to notice what thoughts are no longer serving you and to choose thoughts you want to integrate into your belief system. What messages from childhood are you still carrying? How are they affecting your perception of yourself now in the world? You can begin to change any negative messaging by repetition of positive thoughts. By defining what you would like to believe about yourself, and then collecting evidence daily that supports the desired belief, you'll begin to notice the daily increase of positive evidence. New beliefs about yourself will begin to take root and flourish.

2. You can rewrite your life script by using the tools in this chapter. They can help you write the next best chapters of your life. Dante Alighieri writes, "A mighty flame followeth a tiny spark." You have the power to begin this shift in personal perception and watch the sparks of your new life ignite.

3. When good experiences or feelings happen during your day, pay attention to them and take a breath or two and let them count! As you marinate on what feels good, you start to notice more good things in your life!

4. Trauma is held in the fight or flight part of your brain. Notice if you have a stronger reaction to something than the situation may warrant. If you notice yourself being triggered, you may want to consider doing some EMDR to help rewire those past negative experiences which are also held negative beliefs. You can rewire your brain and enjoy your life more fully.

5. You have the power to change your brain and ad more spark, pleasure and happiness to your life! You CAN do it!

Chapter 2

The Art of Befriending Yourself

"Do you want to meet the love of your life? Look in the
mirror."

—Byron Katie

We've heard messages like these all our lives:

"Love yourself."

"Be your own best friend!"

"You have to love yourself first before you can allow
someone else to truly love you."

But doing this—if you don't know how to, or if you've
never really practiced being kind to yourself—can seem
like a very daunting task. The critical voice that runs
commentary in your head all day can make it very difficult
to like yourself—much less *love* yourself. But this *can* be
done. And it's an essential part of creating a richer, more
fulfilling life.

Loving yourself begins with befriending yourself. This
means treating yourself as you would someone with whom
you were starting a friendship: building trust and learning
how to show up. When you meet someone new, you don't

just instantly trust them to be tuned in to you, to have your back when you're are upset, or to make you a priority in their lives. As you spend time with them and observe that their kindness, compassion, and care are consistent, you learn that you can rely on them to be there for you. You've built a trusting relationship. You can also do that with yourself.

As you make yourself a priority in your own life—showing up to exercise, meditate, eat good foods that nourish your body, and keep your daily commitments to yourself—you'll strengthen the bond with your internal self. You'll start to believe, "I can rely on me! I am truly my own best friend!"

You gain trust with yourself when you:

- Speak your truth
- Nurture your inner creativity
- Focus on what generates happiness in you and make it a part of your daily life
- Use daily self-affirmations to cultivate your strengths and positive characteristics and attributes
- Are gentle with yourself when you make a mistake and use supportive, nurturing language to build yourself back up

I've worked with many men and women in their 30s, 40s—even 50s and beyond—who have said to me, "I don't know who I am or even what my interests are anymore." They've spent so much time fulfilling a role—husband, wife, student, employee, executive, caretaker, or lone wolf—that they've lost the connection to who they truly are. They've lost touch with their inner voice, and now they're desperate to find it.

We all get caught up in the outer world. The mistake so many of us make in seeking fulfillment and identity in life is that somehow, we get fooled into believing that the vast majority of that pleasure, fulfillment, or happiness we're craving is outside of us. We don't learn how to befriend ourselves along the way. All the money, cars, trips, homes, success and fame in the world aren't enough to achieve that true, deep, inner fulfilment. No matter what or who we surround ourselves with, in the end, it's only our voice that's talking in our head at 2 a.m. on a Tuesday morning. We'd better make sure that voice is one that truly loves us and cares about our highest good.

Building a More Positive Inner Image through Affirmations

Start by looking at your self-talk. What are the messages you're giving yourself? A great way to transform this inner voice into a more positive and productive one is to begin working with affirmations.

I know, I know. We all get the picture of Stuart Smalley on *Saturday Night Live* looking in a mirror saying, "I'm good enough. I'm smart enough. And doggone it, people like me!" But Stuart wasn't too far off. The words "I am" are two of the most powerful ones in the English language. Whatever follows those two words, we're actually programing into our minds.

"I am strong."

"I am beautiful."

"I am lazy."

Whatever we attach to the end of "I am" reinforces the way we see ourselves in the world. So, choose your words wisely.

Joel Osteen's "I Am" sermon will rock your soul (and you don't have to be a Christian to get the power of his message). Oprah said that this sermon changed her life, and when I heard that, I had to check it out. It was the first time I'd ever seen or heard of Joel Osteen. His message had me in tears (and I'm not one of those women who cries easily at sentimental movies.) It was just that powerful.

In this sermon, Joel talked about how important it is to notice what you say to yourself when you get out of bed each day, when you look in the mirror, and when you make a mistake. We all know the difference between "I made a mistake" and "I am a mistake" The important thing is to affirm the good in you—whether you believe it fully or not—until it becomes your truth. "I am vibrant. I am healthy. I am more than enough! I am a masterpiece!" You will come away from this practice feeling empowered and able to start working on your own most powerful "I am" statements.

I've found that working with 10 to 15 affirmations a month is truly effective. As I mentioned before, it takes approximately 30 days of daily practice for our brain to form a new thought pattern or behavioral habit. It may take a lot of effort at first, but after 30 days, it's become a routine and a thought habit. You'll begin to automatically go work out or make a healthy choice at a restaurant. You can do this by writing your affirmations in a journal or notebook. I always recommend writing things by hand because it tells our brains, "Hey! Listen up! This stuff is really important!"

After writing your affirmations, say them out loud to yourself each morning. Don't just listen to the words. Envision yourself as the person you're affirming. Be aware of how good these statements feel as you speak them into your life. It's a powerful process that will begin to change how you think and feel about yourself.

I also have my clients check out the Think Up app if they have an iPhone. This is an awesome app that will allow you to pick from a menu of affirmations in a bunch of different life categories. Or you can just write your own. The program has you type or speak your affirmations into the app. Then, it will prompt you with your own words so that you can record your own voice saying what you most need to hear. *And* it will set your voice to music in a continual loop. This is important because we hear our inner critical voice in our heads all day long. So, to hear our kinder, gentler voice telling us a more accurate message about ourselves is very soothing and effective.

Dr. Bruce Lipton told me during our interview that our mind is in theta waves (and most susceptible to input) first thing in the morning and last thing at night. By playing this recording as you fall asleep, it is able to get into your subconscious mind and begin to lay down new habitual ways of thinking and believing. Since 95% of our beliefs are subconscious, this is a great way to get in there and do some subconscious reprograming and replace it with new and improved ways that will lead you to feeling (and thinking) your way into a happier more joy-filled life.

As I said before, an important aspect of doing affirmations is to not only hear them but feel them as you say them. You know how good it feels when someone else affirms you. Saying your affirmations out loud in the morning and putting a hand on your heart as you say them can help them stick and become new habitual ways of developing a positive and improved belief system.

As we affirm something over and over, we engrain it in our memory. We didn't come out of the womb knowing how to tie our shoes or what $2 + 2$ equals. But now, we can do both automatically. When we practice something over and over, what's called a "myelin sheath" builds up over the neuropathway, making it a more automatic response. What once took a lot of conscious effort—like learning to tie our shoes (make the rabbit ears, now loop this one around...)—

has now become totally unconscious. We just do it. It's kind of like how we find ourselves home from the office at the end of the day without really being totally conscious of how we got there. We were on automatic pilot. This is the importance of repetition.

In his book *The Upside of Fear,* Weldon Long tells the amazing story of transformation in his own life. He went from being a 9th grade high school dropout and self-loathing felon who served 13 years in prison, to a truly successful man of high moral integrity.

I was honored to have Weldon as a guest on my show and his story touched me deeply. He discussed how seven years before he was released from prison, he had (unbeknownst to him at the time) what was to be his last phone call with his father. A week later, his father, in his late 50s was dead and Weldon was left with the unshakable thought, "My father was not able to tell me he was proud of me for anything." He felt he had failed his father in every way possible.

This last phone call affected Weldon so profoundly that he decided that he had to become the kind of man his father would have been proud of. When he got off of the phone from hearing the news of his father's death, we walked down the hallway and was drawn to the closet the prison guards stored books in a cardboard box for the prisoners to read. The first book he picked up was Stephen Covey's, 7 Habits of Highly Successful People. He said he went to his cell and he sat down and read the book. It affected him so deeply, he read it again, and again, until he began to incorporate the words in the book into his own belief system. For seven years, Weldon read books on self-improvement, and he learned how to have a success mindset. He earned a degree in business and in law and became a man of faith. Because prisoners aren't allowed to have thumbtacks, he said he had to use toothpaste to hold up his list of affirmations. Repeating them several times a day, he began to "feel into" what it was like to be the man those affirmations described. Weldon not only changed his mind set, but he also rewired his subconscious mind and rebuilt the internal image of who he truly was.

Five years after leaving prison, Weldon became a highly successful businessman and owned a 22 million dollar a year company, had a successful marriage, and most importantly to him, he obtained custody of his 10-year-old son. Today, in addition to having a multimillion-dollar business and national speaking engagements, he's published several books, including the *New York Times* best seller *The Power of Consistency*. By changing his thoughts, he changed his feelings, his actions, and his relationship with both himself and the world.

Cultivating a Relationship with Yourself

We aren't always used to spending time with ourselves. Most of us are used to the art of distraction. We wake up, and we immediately grab our phones to see what text, voicemail, email, tweet, or post has come in. We listen to music and podcasts, or we start running through our daily to-do lists without checking in with ourselves. Yes, you can check your phone briefly. But the first half hour of the day belongs to you. Allow yourself to be the priority in your own life before you start focusing on others.

One of my favorite times of the day is the 10 minutes after I'm fully awake, before I get out of bed. I put one hand on my heart and one hand on my stomach and I feel in full communion with myself. I bring my focus to my heart center and allow myself to connect with my higher power. I let light fill my body. I breathe it in and feel it infuse each and every cell of my body—as if my heart were a sun that spreads love, healing, and radiance throughout my entire being. I silently say what I am thankful for, and I focus on the feeling of deep gratitude in my heart. I also send light and love to those friends, family members, and clients who might be needing some extra support in that moment. I emerge from the covers feeling light, refreshed, and full of joy to start the day.

You can choose a morning routine that works best for you. In his book *The Miracle Morning*, Hal Elrod provides a fantastic format for supercharging the first hour, half hour—or even 10 minutes—of your day. SAVERS is his acronym for Silence, Affirmations, Visualization, Exercise, Reading, and Scribing. He says that even if you did each of these activities for just one minute, you'd set up your day for positivity and success.

For me, the key elements to tuning in to myself in the morning are centering, breath, gratitude, mindset, and movement.

Centering

There are countless ways you can center yourself, and it can be fun exploring what works best for you. How do you connect best with your heart? It might be prayer, meditation, chanting a mantra, or listening to a guided mindfulness practice on YouTube. The method doesn't matter as much as the personal fit. Try different things until you find one that feels right for as long as it's useful. Then, you can move on to a new one.

One of my all-time favorite morning centering practices came from Marianne Williamson's CD *Meditations for a Miraculous Life*. During a certain period in my life, I think I listened to her morning meditation for well over a year, every single morning. It guides you to let go of yesterday, cross the bridge over into today, and start anew. It's beautiful and timeless. It also includes tracks specific to work, relationships, and money.

YouTube has a plethora of offerings if you prefer guided meditation. Other people prefer to listen to their breath or repeat a mantra. A beautiful centering mantra is "I breathe in love," which you say as you inhale, and "love flows out," as you exhale. Allow the words to flow with your breath.

The main point of centering is to get out of your head and into your heart. Spending time getting to know the interior of your heart is an essential part of befriending yourself.

Breath

You can get in touch with your breath through conscious breathing while you're exercising, doing yoga, or even just being more mindful of your breath. The breath is what connects us to our life force, and awareness of our breath going through our bodies is invigorating. I often have clients become conscious of their breath during a session to help them center, relax, or even to help stop an oncoming panic attack.

Here's the process I recommend:

Sit in a chair and close your eyes. Take a deep breath into your belly and slowly release it. Feel yourself begin to relax into your chair and let it support you completely. Take another deep breath—this time all the way down to your kneecaps. As you slowly release it, silently say, "I am calm and relaxed." Now, take one more nice, deep breath— this time, all the way down to the tips of your toes. Slowly release. Allow your awareness to focus on the sensation of your breath at the tips of your nostrils. Notice how cool the air is as it enters your body. Follow the sensation of your breath as you inhale. Notice the sensation of your breath as it touches the back of your mouth or throat. Now, continue to follow that breath. Notice the sensation of your chest rising and falling as your lungs expand and contract with your breath. Then, bring your awareness to the subtle movement of your breath in your abdomen. Notice the rise and fall of your breath. Become aware of the wave of breath as it flows through you. Bring your attention to where you most naturally notice your breath. It may be the nostrils, the back of the mouth or throat, the chest, or the abdomen. Just notice for a moment. Then, allow yourself one more deep, cleansing breath. Slowly open your eyes. You will be feeling more calm, centered, and relaxed.

Gratitude

As far back as I can remember, I feel as if I've been listening to Oprah talk about the benefits of gratitude. Almost 20 years ago, I remember being inspired by her gratitude journal, and that's when I began writing down five things each day that I felt thankful for. I've seen the tremendous power of this practice and mindset in my own life. Remember that when you focus on something it expands? The same is true for gratitude. The more you focus on it, the more reasons you'll have in your life to be grateful. It moves you out of a mentality of lack and into a place of abundance.

In January 2007, I opened the doors to my private practice. I was still working part time as an elementary school counselor, and I wanted to start seeing clients two days per week. Not knowing how to really start my own business, I'd sent out about 50 announcements to different people in the community—doctors, dentists, teachers, realtors— anyone I could think of who might send me a referral. I'd been open a total of two weeks—and it was crickets. I wasn't sure what to do.

I called my father to tell him about my dilemma, and he asked me, "Well, how are you praying for it?" I said, "Well, at this point, I'm asking the universe to please, please, please send me some clients!" He laughed and told me I was going about it all wrong. "While you're on the phone with me right now, I want you to write down 10 times 'Dear God, thank you for sending me (number of) clients.'" He asked me how many clients I wanted, and I said I wanted to start with six. "OK. So, write it down and really feel it like it's already done," he said. So, I did. I wrote, "Thank you, God, for sending me six clients" 10 times, and I felt the gratitude in my heart.

The next day I received my first referral. And the day after that, another one. And the day after that. And the day after that. For four days in a row, I received a new referral each day. And on the last day, I received two. I became a believer.

In the 12 years that have followed, my practice has continued to be full. If someone completes therapy, I know I'll be blessed within the next 24 to 48 hour and that vacant appointment slot will be filled by the next person who is meant to be there.

It's never failed. Gratitude works.

Mindset

I like to share with my clients the concept of "bookends" to their day. The most important times of the day for the brain are the first thing when we wake up in the morning and the last half hour before we go to sleep. This is when our brains are most susceptible to suggestion. Utilizing these times to set intentions for the day, prime your mind for feeling good, and holding peace in your heart as you fall asleep are life changers!

The late Dr. Wayne Dyer, who has been one of my mentors for the last 20 years, said that it's essential that we spend the last five minutes before sleep thinking about something positive because our brains are going to be subconsciously marinating on those thoughts for the next seven to eight hours.

What I've found to be highly effective both in my life and in the lives of my clients is beginning the day by writing down three things I'm thankful for and *feeling* that gratitude in my heart. I like Tony Robbins' formula for this too. In addition thinking of two big things, he advises choosing at least one small thing you are thankful for as well—the blue sky, the warmth of your pillow, hot water—because it's important for the mind to notice not only the big "boom-booms" in life, but also the precious "little things" that make life more wonderful and fulfilling.

At the end of the day, I recommend a simple three- to five-minute exercise that will help prime you to feel good as you go to sleep. Find a small object you can hold in the palm of your hand (such as a special stone, or seashell, or anything that has meaning to you). While holding this object, recall what the best part of your day was. Remember as many details as possible and feel into them.

This process is powerful for two reasons. First, the mind has no concept of time. It experiences any image you bring to it as happening *now*. That's why you can think of something sad that happened many years ago, or something that made you angry months ago, and you can feel that that past emotion in the present moment. It isn't happening now—the mind is just experiencing it that way. The wonderful thing is that you can also enhance positive memories and the feelings connected to them as well. Remembering the best part of your day and re-feeling it allows you to re-experience the joy. It's also like knocking on your Reticular Activating Systems door saying, "Hey! Pay attention! This is important information! Start noticing more of this in my life!"

Second, holding this same object night after night begins to form muscle memory which associates the object with feeling good, thereby reinforcing positive feelings associated with the object itself. Keep your best part of the day object on your nightstand or near your bed where it can be a visual reminder to use it and keep yourself going to bed in a positive state.

I learned one of my favorite morning "bookends" from Tony Robbins at his Unleash the Power Within event this last summer. Tony teaches through engaging the audience to push beyond their limits for 54 hours. We walked on 2,200-degree hot coals, broke through fear patterns, and released old thought habits and behaviors that no longer served us. We sang, jumped up and down, and celebrated the gift of being alive.

My biggest takeaway from this experience was his priming exercise that I do in the mornings. It begins with a yoga breathing technique called "breath of fire," which consists of taking 30 sharp, deep breaths in and out of your nose three times. In between sets, you take a short pause and you begin to feel the tingling and a sense of elevated aliveness in your body. (Helpful hint: Blow your nose before you start. You'll get more air and have less of a mess to clean up afterwards!) After the breathing, bring to mind 3 memories of things for which you're deeply grateful, and think of these things for one minute each. Let each one resonate in your heart. From that place of joy and gratitude, you send that love from your heart out to friends, loved ones, clients, employees, your boss, the barista at the coffee shop you frequent, and anyone else you can think of. Let the love radiate out to your community and beyond to all of humanity. From this place, you've just primed yourself for an amazing state to begin your day!

Tony Robbins has a video of this priming exercise from the actual event I attended in NYC in 2017 on YouTube, so you can experience it in its entirety. When I first saw it, I had to watch it several times before I could get through it without tearing up because doing the priming exercise with Tony live had been such a powerful experience for me. The video captures this extraordinary exercise and its ability to move us into a higher state beautifully.

Movement

Movement can be anything from a full workout in the gym to 30 minutes of yoga or 15 minutes of Qigong. Sometimes, I do a hundred jumping jacks and a few sun salutations just to get my blood moving. Other times, I put on my favorite music and dance for 15 to 20 minutes. It doesn't have to be the same movement every day. It just needs to be movement. Listen to your body. See how it feels each morning, and let it guide you. This also allows your childlike, spontaneous self to emerge, which is amazingly energizing and lifegiving in and of itself.

A 15-minute walk can be transforming and combine mindfulness/centering with movement. Just noticing the sky, the trees, the season, and your surroundings can feed your soul. You're part of this wonderful world. Connecting with nature helps you release the negative ions in your body, which also helps you release stress and negativity.

Feeling the sun or the wind on your face can help you to feel more alive. Allow yourself to go outside and breathe it in.

There are endless research studies on the benefits of exercise. It affects your mood, well-being, physical health, and disposition. Some people get hung up an "all or nothing" mentality around exercise and movement. It doesn't have to be that way. You don't have to label yourself as either an "athlete" or a "couch potato"—there are plenty of points in between those two. I often tell my clients, who may just be starting to consider exercising for the first time (or the first time in a long time) to start with only 10 minutes a day. It is a wonderful place to start, and you can build from there. Lao Tzu said, "The journey of a thousand miles begins with one step." This is true. You just have to take the first step toward where you want to go—and you will get there.

Befriending Your Joyful Essence

Another helpful way to befriend yourself is to start getting in touch with your pure essence. While some people are able to do this through prayer and meditation, there's another way that also really helps me and many others I've worked with.

Find a picture of yourself (if you have one) that was taken any time between birth to about five or six years old, in which captures the sweet, innocent essence of you as a child, shining through. Put that picture on your desk, refrigerator, or bathroom mirror where you can see it daily and affirm to yourself, "This is me!" "I am that loving, joyful essence!" Look into the eyes of your happy self-smiling back at you and embrace this deeper part of who you already are.

Just as you would begin a relationship with another person, you can begin to cultivate a real relationship with yourself. We don't just automatically trust someone when we meet them. We learn to trust them as they show up emotionally for us and we learn we can rely on them to be consistent and caring in our lives. As you "show up" for yourself consistently and do your daily practices, you'll begin to trust yourself more. You will begin to trust yourself to make decisions and exhibit behavior that is truly loving and nurturing towards yourself. By making yourself a priority in your own life, you'll find that you have more to give to others around you and you will have a deeper peace and sense of fulfillment.

In this process, it's important to be gentle with yourself. This isn't about perfection—it's about practice. In the same way that you learn to have boundaries with others, you need to learn to have them with yourself. It's OK to say no when you need to protect your time and energy. Asking yourself, "Does this (activity, commitment, event) serve my highest good?" is important in determining what you should and shouldn't do. It's not selfish to think this way. It's still important, of course, to serve others and be sensitive to their needs and wishes. But you need to tune in to yourself first.

It's like on airplanes when the flight attendant says, "In case of an emergency, an oxygen mask will drop down. Put your own oxygen mask on first." We need to learn how to take care of ourselves before we can truly do a decent job of caring for others. When you start making yourself a priority in your life, you start cultivating a relationship of self-respect and developing a deeper capacity to give.

In his book *Wishes Fulfilled*, Dr. Wayne Dyer talks about our higher self as a spark of God within us. He said this spark, which is a tiny fragment of the creative source of the universe, is located within each of us. It causes our hearts to beat, it makes our hair grow, and we take it for granted. Wayne says that if we can focus on growing this spark within us, it can become the primary force in our everyday life. That if we affirm our willingness to change our concept of ourselves, we can recognize and increase that spark. Then, our higher self can become the guiding light of our lives. This is befriending the true spark—our essence and the God spark—in each one of us.

Even if you have difficulty with the word "God," you may be aware of a higher self or higher consciousness that dwells within you. In befriending yourself, you can add flame to this spark within you and expand your life in miraculous ways.

Befriending Yourself -Top 5 Takeaways

1. Use positive, present tense "I am" statement to start changing your internal dialogue to serve you in befriending yourself. What positive messages does your heart most need to hear? Start affirming that to yourself each day.

2. There is power in consistency. Repeating positive rituals in the morning and at night can help change your brain and change your life. You truly befriend

yourself, when you consistently show up for yourself on a daily basis and make yourself a priority in your own life.

3. You will cultivate a deeper relationship with yourself by building up positive resources through the practices of centering, breath work, gratitude, positive mindset, and movement.

4. Get a picture that captures your joyful essence and put it where you can see it and remember you are that amazing spark!

5. Remember, as you take care of yourself, you actually have more to give! You are worth it!

Chapter 3

The Power of Connection

"Love is our true destiny. We do not find the meaning of life by ourselves alone—

we find it with another."

—Thomas Merton

Now that you're beginning to nurture a friendship with yourself, it's also important to talk about the role other people have in your life. There's nothing like the spark that's created when you connect with another person. You can cultivate your connections and increase the sparks in your life no matter how introverted or extraverted you are.

In today's world, a lot of emphasis is placed on being independent, self-reliant, and self-sufficient. While these are all very important parts of being a mature, heathy human being, they also don't paint the full picture of what creates a happy and fulfilled life. Humans are actually hard-wired for connection—to be interdependent on one another.

In an article in Forbes in 2010, Maia Szalavitz wrote about her research on Russian orphans, and revealed heart-wrenching data regarding a staggering mortality rate and failure to thrive rate for babies who are institutionalized and deprived of touch. But how could simply being in an orphanage kill a baby? "Basically, they die from lack of love," she writes. Maia talked about what happens when infants don't get the physical affection they need. Infants deprived of physical affection show a decrease in the production of growth hormone, a weakened immune system, and often times their bodies just start shutting down. We all need to be touched, we all need interaction, and we all truly need to connect with one another to grow and thrive as individuals.

Hollywood, at times, has glamorized the image of a man as a rugged lone wolf, or "a man who needs no one"—an island. In actuality, when a man or woman has few social contacts or connections, life satisfaction and overall personal well-being are diminished.

There's a spectrum of the amount of contact each human being desires. I've worked with many introverts who say, "Being around people is exhausting!" But an important distinction needs to be made here. Being introverted doesn't mean you don't like being around people, that you have no social skills, or that you don't need others. Being introverted means you get refueled from being alone.

People who are extroverted tend to derive more energy from engaging with others. There is no right or wrong to this. I know and have worked with people on both ends of the spectrum who enjoy a nice blend of alone time and social time.

Most people fall somewhere in-between the two extremes on the introvert/extrovert continuum. No matter where we land, most of us still have a deep desire to be seen, heard, and validated as human beings. We need connection for this to occur. While it's essential to value ourselves and be aware of our inherent worth, we also need interaction and feedback from others to experience ourselves completely.

I've worked with many clients who are at a transitional point in their lives. They've just moved into town, or they've recently married, or they're getting (or have recently gotten) divorced. Regardless of the situation, some change in social surroundings has occurred. Their concerns are about feeling lonely and not knowing how to "plug in" to their community or how to start being more social again.

This isn't easy. As adults, when we don't know people, it can be very intimidating to try to make new friends. Gone are the days of elementary school when we just walked up to Brooke or Bobby and said, "Will you be my friend?"

That was all it took. Recess, tag, and friendship were all sealed in a single transaction. As adults, it feels more awkward. And our minds, which are hardwired to help us steer away from things that are uncomfortable, can lead us down the path of least resistance and coax us to just stay home (or on our side of the "playground").

Also, our minds love predictability. Any time we go into a new situation, the brain puts all systems on high alert, which activates our anxiety. So, we really have to lean into this uncomfortable edge and by-pass our hardwired circuitry if we want to meet new people. There are a couple of helpful things you can do to make entering into new social and interactive situations easier.

Connecting with Affirmation and Visualization

We all have our own comfort zone. Unfortunately, for many people, it's only as large as a step or two out of their front door. I teach clients how to take their comfort zones with them. It starts with creating affirmations specifically designed for confidence and connection. Here are some examples:

"I am comfortable in my own skin."

"I approve of myself and feel comfortable wherever I go."

"I love myself, and I feel love and acceptance from everyone I meet."

"I move through life confidently. I love being a part of the world around me."

Play with this and see what affirmations fit best for you.

Before you go to an event where you know you'll probably be meeting new people, it can be helpful to practice the following visualization:

Visualize your comfort zone as a circle of energy that surrounds you. It's best to close your eyes to do this. The circle can be any color that you associate with comfort, and it can be as big or as little as you need it to be. Imagine that you're breathing in this color. Allow this healing, calming color to fill your lungs, your heart, and your mind. Let it permeate and penetrate each and every cell, filling you with calm, comfort, and confidence.

As you breathe into this circle, imagine it expanding. Visualize a time you felt comfortable in a social interaction. Remember those feelings and bring them into the present moment. Then imagine what it will feel like to interact with others from this calm, confident space. See yourself laughing, being light-hearted and relaxed as you talk with other people. Notice how your comfort zone can expand out to include the person or persons you're interacting with. Allow yourself to breathe in these good feelings. Feel them in your heart-center. You can even put your hand on your heart or solar plexus to ground these feelings in your body. When you're ready, open your eyes, and head to your event. You'll feel grounded in your own good energy, and your mind will be primed for positive interactions with others.

I had a client who was a junior in college at Colorado State University. He had pledged to a fraternity that sent him to a leadership school in Kansas. He was a very sweet, shy young man when I first met him. He blushed easily and had a difficult time speaking up for himself. When he returned from that leadership school, he shared an invaluable tool he had learned there that helped increase his confidence level and, in turn, changed his life.

One of the speakers at the school had told the young men that when they saw someone, they want to meet; they should just do it because they had nothing to lose. He said, "Going into the interaction, you don't know that person, and they don't know you. You're not friends. If you risk extending yourself and just say hi, there's a 50/50 chance that you might strike up a conversation and you will have made a friend. If that person doesn't become your friend, you've lost nothing. They weren't your friend to begin with."

The other part I would add to that "losing nothing" idea is that, if for some reason that person rejects you, they're not truly rejecting *you*. They don't know you! So, all they're really rejecting is an idea of who they *think* you are. This is a projection through their own life lens, which is colored by all of their life experiences and conditioned thoughts. If you think about it, this dramatically minimizes the risk of extending yourself. You truly only have something to gain.

Your Thoughts Impact How You Connect

Most of us have thinking errors (no matter how evolved or aware we are.) These are automatic thoughts that rise from our subconscious—often to protect us—but in the end, they don't end up serving us at all. Common thinking errors are mind reading, minimization, catastrophizing, and all-or-nothing thinking. For a list of the 10 most common thinking errors, google "David Burns cognitive distortions," and you'll start to become aware of which ones you use most frequently.

One of my big thinking errors used to be mind-reading. This is when a person thinks they "know" why another person reacted in a certain way or said certain things. In essence, this is that part of us that makes up the story or fills in the blanks to make sense of things when we don't have all the details. But the truth is, unless you're psychic (and I'm pretty sure you're not, unless you are already receiving paychecks from the Psychic Friends Network), none of us knows what someone else is thinking or why someone acts in a particular way. We're only assuming we know—and you know what they say about assuming!

I remember a time a thinking error really triggered me. I was working at a tough little South Side school in Cheyenne, Wyoming, as a social work counselor. There was one teacher in the Kindergarten class who didn't seem to like me because she didn't greet me in the school hallways when we passed each other. I came up with every possible reason of why she might not like me: "She's threatened by me because other people really like me." "She's stuck up and thinks she's better than me." The list went on and on. Finally, after working there about six months, I went to see her after school to discuss a student we shared. As I entered her classroom, I told the voices in my head that were shouting, "She doesn't like you!" to calm down and be quiet. Ironically, after our conversation about the student, she started opening up about the difficulties in her own life. She shared about her painful marriage, which was crumbling, and the severe depression she was struggling with that made it difficult for her to even hold her head up most days. I had totally misread her. Her behavior had nothing to do with me. I had just internalized it as, "She doesn't greet me because she doesn't like me." It couldn't have been further from the truth.

We went on to become good friends, and I doubt our friendship would have been actualized if I'd continued to be stuck in my mind-reading thinking error.

That was a big "aha" moment for me. I've since become aware of how that specific thinking error and others come up in my life. Clients often ask me if I still get triggered by thinking errors, and I say, "Of course I do!" I'm just able to untwist my thinking more quickly now and move on so that those thoughts don't become mental stumbling blocks for me or barriers to my relationships.

You can learn how to become aware of your own thought patterns and put the "lie to the test" when you find you're thinking negatively. A very helpful question in untwisting your thinking is "What evidence do I have that supports this thought?" If there's little to none, chances are, it's a thinking error.

When clients are struggling with self-image or self-confidence but want to put themselves "out there" and meet new people, I often suggest we set up a kind of social experiment. We start by debunking the client's thinking errors or limiting beliefs that may be connected to meeting people, and we work on replacing them with more accurate ones. Then, I ask the client to consider practicing "putting on" the persona of a confident person for the particular event the client wants to attend—as if they were putting on a certain outfit for the night. I ask them to "try on" feelings of confidence and then see what their experience is like. Often, I have the client close their eyes and recall a situation where they felt confident in the past and work on enhancing the memory and sensations of that feeling, so they are aware that they have the ability to pull up that feeling at will.

We go with this hypothesis: "If I am more confident when I am meeting new people, I will have a positive experience." I ask the client to just collect data that does or doesn't support this hypothesis, which we talk about and process during the following session. It takes some of the pressure off the whole social interaction to frame it in this context.

The results are tremendous. One female client who was afraid to talk to men after her recent divorce (following 15 years of marriage) practiced this "trying on the emotion" technique. She said, "I just walked into the party and thought, "I am an interesting and intelligent person! People would be delighted to talk to me!" And that's exactly what happened. She said at one point she found herself in a doorway talking to two different men at the same time and feeling, "I am the belle of the ball!"

This activity affected her in two powerful ways:

1. It broke through her old belief— "I am awkward and not interesting"—because she had enough evidence in a single evening to disprove it, so she was able to let it go.
2. Because of this single positive experience, she continued to attend social functions and connect and

interact with people with far more confidence and was able enjoy her life more fully.

I encourage you to try out these different techniques and see which ones work best for you. Take your improved relationship with yourself "out on the town," and watch the positive connections grow in your life.

We are All Connected

I had the amazing honor of interviewing Larry Dossey on my show and discuss his book, The One Mind- How Our Individual Mind is Part of a Larger Consciousness and Why it Matters. Larry is a distinguished physician and an international advocate for the role of the mind and spirituality in healthcare. In our interview, he discussed how we are all truly connected and can experience this unity to all of humanity. Through decades of research, fellow physicians sharing their experiences, and his own personal experience, Larry has found scientific evidence that takes us beyond Darwin's theories of survival, a kind of every man for himself, into a realm where we can come to the awareness that we are all a part of each other, and what happens to one of us affects us all.

Larry shared his own story of this as a field medic in Vietnam in 1968 and 1969. As a field battalion surgeon, he was responsible for saving many lives. But the most striking example of this sense of interconnection to others happened when a helicopter crashed, landed upside down, and drenched everybody and everything in gasoline. Larry was close to the crash when it happened. Nobody else would even get close to this crashed helicopter because they knew it was going to explode and they didn't want to get burned up. Despite that, Larry and one of his medics rushed into the helicopter and cut one of the pilots, who was incapacitated, free from his seatbelt and drug him out of the wreckage. Fortunately, the helicopter did not explode.

Larry later pondered the situation and why he had done that. He found, philosopher Author Schopenhauer's writings that discussed how in situations like that, there is no reasoning or logic and that something larger than us takes over and there is no longer separation between ourselves and the other. We become one with the other at that moment and just act. It was as if Larry was not rescuing someone else, he was rescuing himself. He was intimately connected to another human being. This is the one mind in action.

We don't need to be in life or death situations to feel this interconnectedness to each other and to all of life. It is as easy as going into silence and feeling that connection inside of your own heart. There is a wonderful meditation in the Buddhist tradition of practicing loving-kindness which will help you to feel this. It begins with connecting with yourself. As you start this meditation, it can be helpful to put your hands on your heart, and allow the good feelings to permeate your entire being as you repeat:

May I be filled with loving-kindness.

May I be safe from inner and outer dangers.

May I be well in body and mind.

May I be at ease and happy.

You might do this for 5 to 10 minutes. Then, once you have a sense of this loving-kindness for yourself, you can bring to mind others; starting with loved ones and friends, and moving to acquaintances, and then, even to people you are struggling with. Allow the loving feelings continue to radiate out of this heart space as you picture each person and repeat:

May you be filled with loving-kindness.

May you be safe from inner and outer dangers.

May you be well in body and mind.

May you be at ease and happy.

You might even imagine sending out that intent for all of humanity; that everyone would be filled with this loving-kindness. Imagine the world we would live in if that were true! We are all so much more alike than we are different. By taking the time to notice your sense of connection to others and to all of life, not only does a sense of loneliness melt away, but the more you practice feeling loving-kindness towards yourselves and others, the more open you will be to experiencing connection and the more it will show up in your life.

Connection in Action

For three years, I worked with a young boy named Charlie. When I met him, he was 10 years old and had been diagnosed with Asperger's Syndrome. He wasn't able to interact well with others and was truly lacking in social skills. On the playground, Charlie would engage in what is referred to as "parallel play" with the other boys. He could sit near where the other boys were playing ball, but he wouldn't participate. Charlie had a desire to be close to them, so when they were on the basketball court, he'd sit very close to them on the sidelines, and he'd rock back and forth, flapping his hands. Just being beside the other boys gave him a sense of connection that was comfortable for him.

Charlie attended my weekly social skills group at the elementary school, and he worked hard on making eye contact and learning how to engage others in conversation. It was slow progress, but he expressed that he really wanted to have friends, and we continued to work together to improve his communication skills. He had an innate desire to connect and even though his mind may not have been wired for this, his heart definitely was.

Charlie and I formed a meaningful relationship over the next few years. I had recess duty on Tuesday mornings, and on these recesses during his sixth-grade year, I would approach him to see if he wanted to play tag with me and a few of the other kids from his class. He always said, "No. Maybe next time." This went on the entire year—until the week before spring break. I will never forget that beautiful, sunny morning. The air was crisp, and the sky was clear. You could hear the squeaking of the swing sets and the happy yelps and laughter from the children bustling around the playground. That morning, I had Meredith, one of Charlie's classmates with me. As I did each Tuesday morning recess, I went up to Charlie, who was sitting on the ground making mounds with the gravel that covered the playground and asked him if he'd like to play tag. He looked up, squinting because the sun was in his eyes, and this time, to my ultimate surprise, he said, "OK! I will!" He held out his hand, and I pulled him up onto his feet. Then, he exploded at a full run, chasing after us yelling, "I'm gonna get you!" with a radiant smile illuminating his sweet face.

This was just the beginning for Charlie. He continued to develop social and interactive skills, and he grew tremendously in his ability to make connections with others. The last day of school that year, he came into my office to say goodbye. I had a special rock that had been polished into a perfect sphere in my office. He'd always admired it, and I wanted him to have it.

As he held the little stone treasure in his hand, his eyes lit up. He came over, wrapped his small arms around me, and said, "I love you, Miss Stephanie." To this day, I consider it one of the most precious moments in my career.

I kept track of Charlie even after he left elementary school. Over the following years, I'd occasionally meet him at Barnes & Noble for a cup of hot chocolate or go out with him for an ice cream cone. In the summer of 2017, when he was 20 years old and already in college, Charlie came to my 50th birthday party. It was mind-blowing to see him interacting with others. Here was Charlie, once a little boy who could barely make eye contact or speak to other people, driving 40 miles by himself to come to the party, interacting with more than 40 strangers and having a ball.

A few weeks later, Charlie wrote on my Facebook page, "You've always helped me through all the troubles I had in elementary, and you helped me understand how to be compassionate and polite to others. Despite all the hardships I went through, I always listened to the good in my heart. You are like family to me, and I just wanted to say, thank you for everything."

Charlie's deep desire to connect is inherent in all of us, no matter what inner or outer circumstances we face. Reading his message, I thought about how we all have these moments when life catches our breath. We feel the power of connection and realize that something amazing has come full circle. This was one of those moments.

The power of connection is intrinsically connected to our sense of well-being. See where you can start growing these connections, even in the smallest of ways, and watch the happiness and contentment in your life increase daily. Our relationships add sparks to our lives and help us open us up to whole new worlds in each other.

The Power of Connection – Top 5 Takeaways

1. We are all interdependent beings and wired for connection. Our survival as infants depended on contact with others. As you grow up, whether you are and introvert or extravert, connection with others will help you thrive in your life.

2. Positive self-talk and affirming your ability to connect with others can help rewire limiting beliefs and help you to feel more confident in social situations.

3. You can practice feeling comfortable interacting with others by visualizing yourself in positive social situations and feeling into a past sense of confidence. Take time to practice in your mind first and then test the experience in your life. Remember, you lose nothing when you enter social situations and extend yourself to just say, "hi." There is a

50/50 chance you will have gained a friend. Strangers are just friends we don't know yet.

4. We are all connected. Take time to feel your connection with all of life. Practice the loving-kindness meditation to increase this sense of interconnectedness and peace in your life.

5. Just like Charlie, you may feel like you have certain things that stop you from connecting with others in a way you would like to. Take the risk and practice going beyond your comfort zone. As you participate with and connect to others, it will enrich and fulfill your life in amazing new ways!

Chapter 4

Revving Up Your Relationship

"The greatest thing you'll ever learn

Is just to love and be loved in return."

—Eden Ahben

When we think of "sparks" in relationships, we think of that initial chemical reaction we feel when we've met someone new and we're in, what I call, "a high state of like." This is an exciting and magical time in any relationship. But as all long-term couples know, the initial sparks don't last forever. The chemical cocktail we feel when we're first with our partners is like nothing else. We have an enhanced state of awareness, attunement, and interest, which borders on chemical obsession in the brain.

This intensity is meant to fade. It's not sustainable—nor would we want it to be. This doesn't mean the love or interest has faded. It's just how our brains work. Our brains thrive on the familiar and also function on the path of least resistance. It categorizes information so it can function as efficiently as possible with the least effort necessary, so it can get back to its most important job of insuring our survival. As we learn about and become familiar with this other person, our brain begins to categorize our partner and stops being as hyper-attentive as it once was in the beginning. Our partners become automated in the brain just like the many of the other things in our lives do (such as our morning routine or the route to and from work). Think about how much attention you had to use the first time you sat behind the wheel of a car. You were hyper focused on where to put your hands, where the mirrors were, and staying inside the lines. Now, you get to work and say to yourself, "How the heck did I get here!" Your mind has automated the information, so you are just operating on automatic pilot. Relationships are just the same in the brain. After a year or so, our brain has "memorized" a great deal about our partner. So, we have to be much more intentional if we want to keep the sparks flying.

I used to love this bit comedian Eddie Murphy did back in the 80s about relationships. He talked about how when you're first with someone, it's like Ritz Crackers. You think it's the best crackers you ever had in your life. Then, when you get married and you've had the same "crackers" day after day, you wake up one day and say, "This is just regular old crackers."

If we want to have "The Ritz" experience with our partners, we have to work on ways to be present with and intentional about our relationship in order to make it a spark-filled experience.

So, although the initial sparks aren't sustainable, creating new sparks and deeper connection is possible. Cultivating a deeper relationship, focusing on giving to one another, and continuing to create fun and novelty in our relationship—as we did when we were first dating—will get us a relationship that continues to grow more fulfilling and delicious with time.

The Communication Gap

I've heard it said that sex and money are the biggest complaints between couples. What I've found in my work with couples is that while sex and money may be issues, the underlying, bigger issue is always communication.

Many couples struggle with expressing their feelings to one another and feeling safe enough to bring up certain topics. I constantly hear couples say they didn't bring up what they really wanted to talk about because they didn't want to rock the boat when they were getting along really well, or things were just too tense to bring it up, and there never becomes a "good time" to just talk. But continued lack of communication begins to create resentment and distance. Even really good couples can have stumbling blocks in talking with and understanding one another. If they let this go unattended, they begin to erode the foundation of their relationship.

Communication is a miracle. Considering the fact that each of us experiences and interprets the world through an individual lens that's colored by each of our own personal histories and past experiences, it's a miracle that we can understand each other at all! But enhancing communication skills is both absolutely doable and essential to increased understanding, compassion, connection, and empathy with each other in this ever-changing world.

In most couples, there are two kinds of people. Harville Hendrix, who has devoted his professional career to helping heal the world one couple at a time, states that there are turtles and there are hailstorms. These are two ways people behave when conflict arises. The turtle is the person who goes inward or has a "flight" response to stress. This person needs time to process emotions internally and, then, when it feels safe, can come back out to talk about them.

The hailstorm, on the other hand, is the person who wants to talk about the conflict *right now*, while it's happening. This person has a "fight" response to stress and feels that if the problem is talked about right then and there, it can be solved. Unfortunately, the hailstorm also thinks that if it just follows the turtle around and hails on it a little bit longer, then the turtle will come out of its shell. Actually, the opposite is usually true. The harder the hailstorm hails, the more deeply the turtle will retreat into its shell. At that point, communication comes to a standstill. If the hailstorm can learn to back off a little bit and tolerate the anxiety that comes with not immediately trying to solve the problem, the turtle can retreat, process feelings, and then when it feels safe enough, emerge again to communicate and connect more effectively.

I once worked with a couple who embodied this analogy perfectly. Mathew was the hailstorm, and Janet was the turtle. Every time the two of them would get into an argument, she'd try to retreat to the bedroom or bathroom; he'd follow her unrelentingly around the house, often cornering her in one of the rooms. The argument would often escalate from there.

During a particularly heated session in my office one day, they discussed the details of a huge fight they'd gotten in the night before. Both of them were in their 40s, but when they got into a fight, all gloves were off, and it was like dealing with a couple of ticked-off teenagers. Apparently, Mathew had followed Janet around "hail storming" during the argument (even though we'd been working on boundaries). And she, turtling up and avoiding him, finally had nowhere to go, so she locked herself in the bathroom and decided to cool off in the shower. Well, this angered Mathew even more. He felt if he just kept hailing Janet would come out of her shell and finish the fight. What ended up happening is that Mathew got so ticked off about not having a turtle to hail on that he picked the lock on the bathroom door, went over to the shower, according to Janet, "swung open the curtain, farted in the shower, and then swung the curtain shut, just for effect."

After they told me this story, it was crickets in my office for a full minute. Total silence while they waited for my response. The tensions in the room were thick and mounting. With an completely expressionless "therapist" face, I turned to Mathew and said, "Mathew, I was wondering if next time you're feeling upset, you'd be willing to just use words, instead of gas, to communicate your feelings." We all looked at each other wide-eyed for a moment and then everyone burst out laughing. This broke the tension in the room, and they went on to really process and further understand the roles they both took on and had a very transformative session.

After this heightened experience of how they embodied the roles of the hailstorm and the turtle, Janet and Mathew were finally able to see the absurdity of their behavior. They started choosing different ways to calm down and later truly connect when they got caught in these rolls. Janet and Mathew learned how to communicate at a more open-hearted level, and they were able to have a much safer, more connected, and more supportive relationship.

One important note. When a couple is in the heat of the moment and one or both are triggered, this is generally not a good time to communicate. It takes a minimum of 20 minutes for our blood pressure, heart rate, and cortisol levels to return to baseline. When a fight-or-flight response gets out of hand, I tell couples to take a two-hour break from each other. As Einstein said, "We cannot solve our problems with the same thinking we used when we created them."

It serves you and your relationship well if you can both agree to take a time out if either person gets triggered. This doesn't mean avoiding the issue. I think it can be helpful to say, "I'm really ticked right now (or I am really triggered) and I need to chill out. Can we try talking about this again in a couple of hours?" You can make a point of letting your partner know you think this is important to talk about. You just want to be in a place where you can respond appropriately, instead of merely reacting.

The Art of Apology

Dr. Harriet Lerner, psychologist and author of the *New York Times* best sellers *Dances of Anger* and *Dances of Intimacy*, discussed her more recent book, *Why Won't You Apologize: Healing Big Betrayals and Everyday Hurts*, with me on my podcast. It will go down as one of my favorite interviews.

An expert on relationships, Harriet defined what an authentic apology sounds like and what constitutes a bad apology. She also helped to deepen my understanding of the definition of "forgiveness."

In an authentic apology, the wrongdoer needs to communicate to the injured person that they (a) take full responsibility and own their poor behavior, (b) were truly sorry for the hurt caused, and (c) will work hard not to repeat the hurtful deed.

In an inauthentic apology, the wrongdoer says, "I'm sorry you feel that way." Or uses the word "but"—for example, "I'm really sorry I snapped at you, but you didn't take the garbage out." This kind of apology blames the person who is feeling hurt. Another inauthentic apology is when the wrong doer discounts the hurt person's feelings further by saying, "You're just being oversensitive. It's not a big deal."

Harriet shared that wrongdoers often can't apologize because they don't have a solid platform of self-worth to stand on. Because of this, apologizing threatens to dismantle their fragile ego. They're afraid they'll lose themselves if they admit they're wrong, and they risk feeling shame and a diminished sense of self-worth. Owning up to doing something wrong and saying sorry is extremely difficult for them.

Perhaps the greatest thing I learned from my interview with Harriet was that we don't have to give "full pardon" forgiveness in order to let go of the hurt and heal when someone has wronged us. She explained that you don't need to forgive someone who has never admitted to what they have done, shown remorse, or apologized. Harriet said that if we push people to forgive a wrongdoer who has never shown remorse, we're actually isolating and possibly reinjuring the wronged party. With respect to the myth of this "all or nothing" forgiveness, she said that it's possible to forgive someone 90 percent or 2 percent, let go of the anger and hurt of the incident, and fully heal. She gave the example of a couple she'd worked with after the husband had had an affair on his wife. In therapy with Harriet, they dealt with the affair and did great work to heal their relationship and put their lives back together. A couple of years later, when the husband asked his wife if she'd totally forgiven him for what had happened, she said, "I forgive you 95 percent. I've seen all the hard work you've done in our relationship. But I'll never forgive you for sleeping with that woman in our bed while I was out of town and dealing with my dying father."

This kind of forgiveness makes sense to me. The wife was able to let go of the hurt and anger and to live in a loving, present-focused relationship with her husband. *And* it was

OK for her to hold on to the part that was truly unforgivable.

We can learn this art of apology and forgiveness, and we can allow it to both enhance our communication and deepen our relationships with one another. This is just one of the many tools that will help us grow individually and in loving relationship with our partners.

Enhancing Communication

The prayer of St. Francis includes an important message for communication. It encourages us to seek to understand before we're understood. I encourage couples to do this through what I call "open-hearted listening." When one person needs to talk about an important issue or important feelings, I ask them to invite their partner into conversation using this open-hearted communication technique.

The way you engage your partner when you want to resolve a problem or talk about difficult feelings is critically important. We all know what it feels like when someone says to us, "We need to talk." All the sirens start going off in our heads, and the message that most of us see flashing in our minds is "I'm in trouble!" In our pasts, the person who usually used that sentence was one of our parents because we'd done something wrong, and the feeling of dread when we hear it can get triggered immediately.

A much more benign way of inviting our partners into conversation is to start with something like, "I'd like to connect with you. Is now a good time?" This keeps our partner's brains from jumping into a state of "high alert." I emphasize the importance of asking if it's a good time for the person we want to connect with because the goal of the interaction is connection and understanding. We want that other person to be able to show up emotionally and be present with us in the conversation. If the other person has had a bad day, is tired, or is not in the emotional space to connect, we won't have our needs met for connection. It's better to gather that information beforehand to determine if it's the right time for the conversation or not. If the person you want to connect with isn't in a good space, it's better to ask when a good time to connect would be (and then plan, if possible, to connect within the next 24 hours).

When both parties agree to have the conversation, there need to be ground rules in order for open-hearted communication to occur. Both have to agree to leave their egos checked at the door. This means, "I will be conscious of staying out of my ego, and I am willing to be here and be open to what you have to say, even if it feels uncomfortable." I ask clients to practice getting out of their heads and moving their energy into their hearts when they agree to have this kind of communication with one another. The goal here is understanding and connection—not who is right or wrong. I also remind them that they don't have to agree. It's about practicing the art of active listening and developing the skills to be open to another human being's experience that may be different from one's own.

It's important to take turns speaking and listening without interrupting one another. Allow the person who requested the conversation to go first. Just listen. Put yourself in the other person's shoes to imagine what it would be like to experience what they're communicating. Put on their lens as much as possible while they're talking. Then, reflect back what you heard to make sure that the same message is that being is accurately being received.

I can't believe how many times in my office one person has felt that they communicated their thoughts and feelings clearly to their partner, only to have their partner completely misinterpret where they were coming from.

A perfect example of this is a couple who came to me for therapy after a huge argument the weekend before. Both in their mid-30s, this couple had gone to an amusement park and had gotten into a big fight right in line for the rollercoaster. She wanted to go on the ride, and he was refusing to go with her. The more she begged, the more he held his ground. "But you've been on rollercoasters with me before! Why won't you come with me on this one! You're no fun!" she argued. "This ride isn't safe, and I don't care what you say. I'm not going! You're the one that's not any fun!" he retorted. And the argument got bigger from there.

When we were able to sit down together in my office and process what had happened using open-hearted listening, they were both able to move into a more empathetic place where true understanding and connection began to occur. Communicating from this place changed everything. She was able to communicate her feelings of longing for connection with him, her deep love and excitement for riding rollercoasters, and her desire to experience that same thrill with him that they'd shared years before. He was able to communicate that from his lens (as a structural engineer), going on a 50-year-old wooden rollercoaster hadn't felt safe to him and had made him anxious. He'd wanted to connect with her and had been willing to do so on other rides, but he'd just had a strong reaction to that particular rollercoaster.

The bottom line: It was the exact same ride. Was either of their perspectives or emotional experiences of the situation wrong? No. They just had different perceptions of the rollercoaster. When they could each step away from needing their own personal experience to be right and the other person's to be wrong, they were able to communicate their feelings, reconnect, and have a deeper appreciation for each other's perspective.

This idea of "putting on" the other person's life lens is an important one. In *The Five Love Languages*, Gary Chapman talks about partners can define their love language(s) so that they can connect more deeply with each other. He says that most people try to show love to their partners the way that *they* want to be loved, not necessarily the way that their partners need to have love shown to them. The golden rule in relationships is not "Do unto others as you would have them do unto you." It is "Do unto others as they would wish to have done unto themselves." A very different message.

Chapman's five love languages are: Words of Affirmation, Quality Time, Acts of Service, Physical Touch, and Gifts. It is helpful to think of them as spoken languages. If one of you speaks Spanish and the other Swahili, you're going to have a difficult time understanding each other. More importantly, you'll miss out on the opportunity to express love to each other in the way each of you needs.

My boyfriend and I are perfect examples of this. I'm a "quality time" person and he is an "acts of service" guy. I need uninterrupted face-to-face time with my partner. If my partner is spending time talking, playing a game, dancing, or exploring the world with me, I feel loved and important. For my boyfriend, if his partner is helping him with a project, picking up his laundry from the cleaners, or fixing him dinner, he feels loved.

It wasn't natural for us to "speak" the other person's love language. We both took the 5 Love Languages® Quiz, and then worked on ways to show each other love in the ways we each needed. This continues to enhance our relationship to this day. We're still working on attuning to each other daily as we keep growing as a couple. The truth is, most people have a little of all of the five love languages as ways they liked to be loved. But everyone has a primary love language that really makes them feel seen, appreciated, and validated. You can go online at www.5lovelanguages.com and take a quick assessment to find out your and your partner's love languages and enhance your relationship today.

Emotional Deposits

Along these lines of finding out how your partner likes to be shown love, I often tell couples about the importance of making a daily deposit in each other's "emotional bank account." Yes, we are busy. Yes, we have distractions with kids and jobs and finances and extracurricular activities. But if we don't invest in our relationships daily, it's like not brushing your teeth day after day; if we ignore them, eventually, they will go away.

It's always bothered me when I hear people say, "Relationships are hard work." The truth is, being single is hard work. Meeting people is hard work. Just living life can be hard work! I prefer to use the term "intentional" in reference to the work we do in relationships. Yes, of course, relationships can be hard work at times. But they can also be the most joyful, intimate, exciting, life-giving experiences in the world. It just takes intention.

I often think of an article I read years ago about relationships. This line stood out to me: "You had better notice your wife and tell her that she's beautiful as she goes out the door, or someone else will." *You* want to be that "someone" noticing and speaking up first. When you learn your partner's love language and what lights them up, you can tune in to that and make sure you're making daily deposits to keep that emotional bank account full. When our emotional bank accounts are full, we're more compassionate, empathetic, and easygoing with each other. We feel happier and feel more fulfilled in life. We're able to find true connection when we see, hear, and tune in to each other. You don't want to get to a bump in the road with your partner, only to realize there is nothing left in the account because you neglected to make your daily deposits. It's best to have lots of reserves where this bank account is concerned.

I've seen couples be transformed by the simple act of saying three appreciations to each other every night before bed. Being intentional isn't hard. It just takes intention! Even after a week of practicing appreciation, couples come back and report that they felt more love, connection, and joy in their relationships because they felt "seen" by their partners. They made noticing each other and the relationship a priority. They put nightly deposits in each other's emotional bank accounts.

Re-Visioning and Re-Romanticizing

No matter how long you have been with your partner, because of the law of familiarity, you can get caught up in life, lose the spark, and feel more like roommates than lovers. In the law of familiarity, no matter how amazing, beautiful, or intelligent your partner is, once you're around them for an extended period of time, that newness wears off a little, and the relationship doesn't seem to have the same energy. It's a natural process—and inevitable in all relationships.

Re-visioning your relationship is a powerful tool to help keep essential energy flowing in a positive direction. I remember hearing, if you imagined your partner laughing, happy, at his or her best, or maybe think of an amazing moment the two of you shared, for just one minute a day, it would absolutely change your relationship for the better. What we focus on expands. Focusing on what you like about your partner, rather than what you don't like, is a powerful tool.

You may get really bogged down in what you don't like or wish you could change about your partner. Initially, everything about them was new and interesting. Now you just wish they'd quit leaving their dirty clothes on the floor and their coffee cup on the counter. Re-visioning can help the two of you maintain a positive set point in your relationship; one that you continue to return to that reminds you what you want to focus on, and what you focus on, you will see more of.

Although the one minute a day of positive partner imagery is wonderful, it's probably going to take a little more than that to reignite the sparks. One of the effective tools I've learned is to reimagine the way you'd like your relationship to be.

Set aside around an hour for this activity. Separately, each write down a list of how you'd like the relationship to look in six months to a year. This can be activities you'd like to do together, ways in which you'll communicate more effectively, or ways which you'll increase the intimacy between the two of you. Write it using positive, present-tense language. For example, "We enjoy long walks together each evening." "We listen with open hearts to one another and have great communication." Thursday nights we go out and do something new each week." "We make time to connect intimately and have sex at least three times a week." Do not write: "We won't be so absorbed in our work week and not have time for each other." Our mind thinks in pictures, so we need to be picturing what we *do* want—not what we don't.

What is it you want to create in your relationship? Once you both have your lists, sit down together. Using open-hearted communication, each person listens to the other's list and then repeats back what they heard. Then together, discuss and write down a joint vision that you both agree to work toward together.

I encourage couples to hang this list in their bedroom or on their bathroom mirror and to read it daily as a reminder to be intentional about making this vision a reality. Some couples really get into it. They print out their list, add graphics or pictures, and even laminate it. Just be creative and have fun with this exercise.

Then, take this list and put it into action. Start being spontaneous with one another, be creative in the activities you do together, and try new things. Even though it only takes one person to be intentional in breaking the habits of a stale relationship, with combined efforts, you can have even greater results in enhancing your relationship and creating a much more fulfilling life with one another.

In the end, the quality of our intimate relationships affects the way we interact with the rest of the world. If our relationships are negative and emotionally draining, we have little energy left for creating positive, live-giving relationships outside of that partnership. If we put effort and energy into our primary relationship, the benefits ripple out in concentric circles the way they do when a pebble is thrown into a pond. We feel nurtured, supported, seen, and loved. And we're able to share ourselves in more positive ways with the bigger world. A wise investment, indeed.

Becoming Experts about Each Other

Dr. Stan Tatkin is a clinician, a teacher, and the developer of A Psychobiological Approach to Couple Therapy® (PACT). He also has a great TEDx talk about relationships, which opens with "Relationships are difficult. There is actually nothing more difficult on the planet than another human being." He goes on to explain how the brain works and why, after the chemicals we're flooded with in early courtship are gone, we're left with a brain that has automated our partner into procedural memory. As we talked about before, in essence, this means that no matter how beautiful or wonderful our partners are, eventually, once we're around them enough, our brains no longer perceive them as novel. We're used to them, and they've become predictable to us. It's at this stage that intention in the relationship becomes important. In order to "see" your partner, more effort is required.

The Beatles said, "All you need is love." Well, actually, it ends up that we need just a little bit more than that. We need the skills that help us communicate with and understand one another—skills that come from spending time with, attuning to, and deeply knowing another human being. The journey of intimacy is one of the most challenging and the most rewarding journeys we'll make in our lives.

When Stan was a guest on my radio show and podcast, I was thrilled to connect with him and learn more about the inner workings of relationship from this wise and loving teacher. One of the things that struck me in our conversation was how he helped normalize some of the things we may perceive as negatives in our relationships.

Stan talked about how people might worry about being "high maintenance" in a relationship. But the reality is that we're *all* high maintenance deep inside. If we don't seem it yet, we will be. A little bit of illness or loss is all it will take. We all need to be noticed and cared about—and that takes maintenance. It's OK to have needs in relationships. We need each other. But it is important to note, needing each other doesn't make us needy. We are interdependent beings.

He also said that everyone is annoying at times. Your partner annoys you, and you annoy your partner. This isn't a sign that you shouldn't be together. Stan said it usually takes a year to truly acclimate to another person. He said, "No matter how difficult you think your partner is, you're no piece of cake. If you want easy, get a sea monkey or a chia pet; people are difficult."

My greatest takeaway from that interview was that we can become experts about our partner. We can become our partner's "whisperer" by learning the things that help us handle our partner's moods, reading our partner's intentions, and meet our partner's needs. As we do this, we grow great self-esteem at being good managers of each other. We know how to care for each other in ways that our own parents may not have been able to.

We need to keep putting intention into the relationship without the expectation of what we're going to get back. Part of taking responsibility for who we are and for our own experience is giving to our partner simply because it feels good to give. We're all naturally egocentric, and it takes intention to go beyond our hardwired, threat-scanning brain to be intentional in our giving of love. The good news is that we can learn how to take care of ourselves *and* our partners simultaneously.

It's about being able to see our partner with fresh eyes and not just letting our brain automate that person (which, again, the brain will always do no matter how wonderful our partner is). Attentiveness and presence are the only antidote to this problem. When we can be in the present moment with our partners, focus on them, and look deeply within their eyes, we can restore a sense of novelty, excitement, and connection with one another. It's curative. It's transformative. When we become experts about one another, the longer we are together, the greater the gifts of attention and intention become in our relationship.

Stan shared, "It's the day-to-day small deeds. It's the day-to-day gestures. It's the proof, day-to-day, that we are each other's defenders, keepers, and [that we] have each other's backs…[and as we work on] making that clear every day…that begins to develop a different kind of love that is far deeper, far more lasting, and is hard to compete with."

As you look at your relationship, you have to ask the big question: "Why are we doing this?" You need to know that it's more than just lust and someone to keep you company. We are each other's keepers. Creating a love that's filled with respect, loyalty and devotion—one in which both people are all in—is a mutual investment whose rewards are priceless.

You can re-create and rev up your relationship. With presence and attention, you can generate excitement and novelty. Together, you and your partner can thrive and care about each other in ways nobody else can. The sparks of your relationships aren't just created in the first phase of your relationship. You can ignite those sparks with the power of your intention at any moment.

Revving Up Your Relationship – Top 5 Takeaways

1. The initial sparks of your relationship will eventually fade as you get more comfortable and used to your partner. This will always happen. You can create the life you want together through focusing on your relationship and putting daily

intention in it and depositing into each other's emotional bank accounts.

2. Learn each other's love language. Practice the new golden rule of, "Do onto your partner what they would want done onto them." The assessment is available at www.thefivelovelanguages.com.

3. Learning open hearted communication will help you to better communicate with your partner. When you listen for the goal of understanding and connection, not who's right or wrong, you will open up the doorway to deeper connection.

4. The art of a genuine apology is one where you own your part in what happened and verbalize it to your partner. Instead of using language that blames your partner or gets you off the hook, use language like, "I can see I really hurt you when I showed up late and you were waiting for me. You are important to me and so is your time. I will really be aware of this and truly pay attention to being here on time."

5. You can re-vision and re-romanticize your relationship together. Creating a mutual vision that you both agree you want your relationship to look like, and reading it daily, will help create the

relationship you truly desire. Reignite the spark in your love life!

Chapter 5

Healing through Grief—and Beyond

"Grief is not a disorder, a disease, or a sign of weakness. It is an emotional, physical, and spiritual necessity; the price you pay for love. The only cure for grief is to grieve."

—Earl Grollman

You may be wondering, "What does grief have to do with living a spark-filled life?" Often people want to distract themselves from this feeling or avoid it at any cost. However, feeling your grief is actually an essential part of the process to being able to be a channel that's clear enough to ignite the sparks within you. Allowing the grief process take place when it is present, will allow your inner phoenix to arise from the ashes of the pain you are feeling, and your life will be transformed in positive ways.

I had a client tell me that feeling depressed was like being an insect caught in tar. We worked together on changing her metaphor from an insect just caught in the tar to that of a caterpillar that when stuck, built a cocoon around itself and eventually emerged a radiant butterfly. She loved that image and said it actually gave her hope that she wouldn't be stuck in her grief and depression until it ultimately destroyed her. She understood that being with her grief (building the cocoon) enabled her to be transformed and emerge as a lovelier version of herself.

Loss and grief are important—but not always comfortable subjects to talk about. Because we're hardwired to avoid pain, choosing to look directly at or be with those feelings of loss can seem very counterintuitive. We don't always readily embrace our dark or negative feelings because— let's face it—they don't feel good!

No one wants to feel sadness or despair or emotional pain at any level. But the truth is, if you can acknowledge and embrace these feelings as they occur, you'll move through the healing process more quickly. It's when we deny our feelings that we struggle even more intensely with them.

One of my favorite poems about embracing our emotions is by Rumi, a 13th-century poet.

The Guest House

This being human is a guest house.
Every morning a new arrival.

A joy, a depression, a meanness,

some momentary awareness comes

as an unexpected visitor.

Welcome and entertain them all!

Even if they are a crowd of sorrows,

who violently sweep your house

empty of its furniture,

still, treat each guest honorably.

He may be clearing you out

for some new delight.

The dark thought, the shame, the malice.

meet them at the door laughing and invite them in.

Be grateful for whatever comes.

because each has been sent

as a guide from beyond.

This poem really speaks to the importance of inviting in whatever "shows up at our door," whether it be a joy or a sorrow. It's about allowing ourselves to acknowledge and feel whatever emotions show up for us in our lives.

There's wisdom in our pain. There's a chance for deeper growth than we ever knew was possible. If we allow ourselves to grow through our grief, we can discover the diamonds that lie in wait underneath the pain.

Loss comes in many forms. Not only do we grieve when someone we love dies, but we can also grieve the changes in our lives—as our children grow up and leave home, as our bodies change and we age, and as we transition through life, sometimes leaving jobs, friends, and places that were familiar to us. All of these transitions involve loss. And all loss involves a grieving process.

Even when the change is positive, we may experience some transitionary grief. I remember when I took my 18-year-old daughter (at the time) to orientation at Colorado State University before her freshman year. They gave all the parents a book on transitions, in which there was a sentence that has always stayed with me: "Even when the change is positive—like getting a new job, or getting married, or going to a new school—in the transition, there is often grief for what was left behind: your life before the change."

As we encounter these new, positive changes in our life, we also have to let go of the self we once were—or the life we once had. Change is inevitable, and it can be a wonderful thing. It's also important to honor that what we've given up in order to move to a new place in our lives. This may evoke some feelings of grief in us as we acknowledge this, but it will also allow us to experience more joy as we transition to the new place, we find ourselves in.

When we're with our emotions as they arise, we move through them. When we suppress our emotions, they're stored within us, which inevitably just causes us more pain. I remember Wayne Dyer saying, "Disease is just dis-ease in the body." When we repress our emotions or shove them down saying, "I don't want to feel this way!" we create this "dis-ease" in our bodies.

I love Tara Brach, who is another great author, spiritual teacher, and presenter. She has a wonderful acronym that helps people befriend their emotions when they come up. The acronym is RAIN, and it stands for:

> **R**ecognize what is going on
>
> **A**llow the experience to be there, just as it is
>
> **I**nvestigate with interest and care
>
> **N**ourish with self-compassion

When we recognize our emotional experience, we're tuning into what's truly going on inside of us. This can help us relax and feel more at ease. Life is amazingly distracting, and it can keep us so busy that we don't make time to tune in to ourselves. So, the first step is to pause, take a deep breath, and recognize what feelings are arising in you.

"Naming is taming" is a great phrase that can help us remember this. Simply naming the emotion arising in us gives us a degree of distance from it. We can observe it a bit more easily. For example, "I am feeling anxiety" is very different from "I am anxious." One means "I am experiencing a feeling," and the other means "I *am* that feeling." So, as we name the feeling, we allow ourselves to identify it as a temporary emotional experience. Naming it, alone, can decrease its intensity.

The allowing of our feelings can actually be the most difficult part of this process. Many people don't want to experience their feelings, and they'll continue to distract themselves through eating, or getting busy doing projects, or shopping, or drinking, or doing drugs. All of these temporary fixes may feel good at the moment, but in the end, they won't serve us, and the pain will still be there waiting for us when we're done being distracted.

It can be very helpful to just breathe into the feeling and notice where it is in our body. When we breathe into that area, the energy we're feeling often moves or changes, and eventually it begins to dissipate. Often, with just the first two steps of recognizing and allowing, we begin to feel relief.

Investigating with interest and self-care doesn't mean rationalizing or analyzing our feelings. We can begin by opening our heart and, with kindness and gentleness, ask, "What does this feeling want from me?" "What am I believing?"—knowing that our thoughts are just thoughts and not necessarily the truth of who we are or the reality of the situation. We tend to judge what's happening, and we have a natural resistance to uncomfortable feelings or pain. If we just make "room" for them by holding them in awareness, we can begin to see that they're momentary thoughts or feelings. We don't have to continue to identify with them or allow them to define us in any way. It's just like watching a beautiful blue sky and observing the white clouds that appear and then fade away. So, it is with our thoughts.

Nourishing yourself with self-compassion is a way to help yourself return to the present moment. By speaking gently and lovingly to yourself (as you would speak to a child who was experiencing the same hurts or challenge), you can dissolve the harsh critic in your head and return to a more peaceful state. Just putting your hand on your heart and breathing into your heart space will help you soothe and calm the raw edges of your experience. If you want to enhance the feelings of self-care and love, close your eyes and imagine a time someone really showed up for you and was very loving and compassionate. As you focus on these memories, you re-create the feelings associated with them, and this will enhance your sense of well-being.

Even when you go through huge challenges, such as a divorce or other major losses, you can continue to practice the RAIN process over and over as new situations or triggers arise. It's a practice. It's not about perfection. And the more you practice being with your shadow feelings, the less afraid you'll be of them. The more you begin to embrace them as being a part of your human experience, the more you'll increase your sense of peace.

The Tough Stuff

I've sat with parents who have lost their children to drug overdose, car accidents, and plane crashes. It is a gut-wrenching process to witness their excruciating pain. There's no "quick fix" to this kind of pain. It's a moment-by-moment experience, and sometimes the best you can do is just breathe through it with no expectation of feeling any different or better. You just have to be with wherever you are in the moment and however you feel at the time.

There's a lovely children's book called *Tear Soup,* by Pat Schwiebert and Chuck DeKlyen. It's written for children, but it's wonderful for anyone of any age because it has universal messages. The book is about an old woman who has suffered a loss (which is never specifically identified) and she's making her own "tear soup" to deal with her grief process. She has to add ingredients every day and keep stirring the soup until it's done. But those around her—who are having a hard time with her sadness—are urging her to get the soup done more quickly. Friends of hers stop coming around because they're tired of her making the soup. But it is her soup and hers alone. Only she will know when it's done.

I think this book is beautiful because it gives each person permission to have your own timetable on our grief journey. No one can dictate to you the time it should take to "get over" a loss. Others may be uncomfortable with your grief, but you need to work through it in your own way—and in your own time.

It's also important to communicate to others where you are at in our grief process so that they know how best to support you. This may change daily or even from moment to moment. That's OK. You need to make sure you're not slipping into a long-term depression and isolating yourself or shutting down. You can keep yourself from going down the rabbit hole by telling others what you need from them, how you need them to give you space or show up for you— even if it feels uncomfortable.

Sometimes we just need someone to listen. Sometimes we need a break from our grief by going out and doing something enjoyable. Sometimes we need time alone to cry, pray, and reflect. These are all important parts of the process of healing. Joining a grief support group can be amazingly helpful in allowing us to heal as we share and connect with others who are experiencing similar feelings. This can help us not feel so alone in our grief experience.

Elisabeth Kübler-Ross, a Swiss-American psychiatrist, first identified the five stages of grief in the late 1960s. Although she listed them chronologically as denial, anger, bargaining, depression, and acceptance, through my work with grieving individuals over the last three decades, I'm aware that these stages don't always happen in a specific order. Frequently, the person grieving will circle back and re-experience stages in no particular order until that stage feels complete.

On my weekly radio show, one of my most powerful interviews was with Tad and Jona Johnson, who had lost their 19-year-old daughter Alexa five years earlier in a single-car accident. Alexa hadn't been wearing a seatbelt, and when she overcorrected while she was driving down I-25 at two o'clock in the morning, her truck started flipping over. She was ejected a hundred yards from her vehicle— the length of a whole football field. Alexa died instantly.

Their story is hard to hear. The depth of pain and the loss they still deal with on a daily basis is palpable. Alexa is also survived by her brother, who was nine years old at the time of the accident, and still grieves with his parents and longs for his sister to be a part of his growing up.

But this story is also one of beauty and hope in healing because of what has happened as a result of this tragedy. In the moments of despair following the news from the state troopers of his daughter's death, Tad stayed awake all night. He was still sitting by the computer where he'd been for almost 24 hours, unable to break away as he collected as many of the photographic images of Alexa he could find on Facebook. As Alexa's friends heard the news of her death, they began sending pictures of themselves with Alexa to her Facebook page. Tad said that the most constant comment he received from her friends was that they would miss Alexa's smile and her laughter, but most importantly, they would miss Alexa's hugs. They said when Alexa hugged them, they would feel it all the way through their hearts.

That next morning, Tad noticed something. In all of the pictures that he'd received of Alexa and her friends, there were several taken in cars. In those pictures, not a single kid was wearing a seatbelt. It was at that moment that Tad put his right hand on his left shoulder and his left arm around his waist, looked up, and said aloud, "Alexa! What are we going to do?" The answer was immediately clear. Tad realized that the way his arms were wrapped around his body was just like a seatbelt hold him. At the same time, he felt a deep warmth come over him like a wonderful hug from Alexa herself.

Immediately, he began to message all of her friends and told them to send him a picture of themselves buckled up in their cars. He told them to imagine they were getting a hug from Alexa as they put on their seatbelts because she would want them to be safe. The pictures poured in. And Alexa's Hugs was born.

Tad and Jona created Alexa's Hugs, a nonprofit foundation that focuses on safety awareness. Their message has been brought to schools, business, and six countries worldwide, and has impacted thousands of teens and adults alike. Alexa's brother Isaac often speaks to rooms of 1,200 teens, sharing his experience of the journey. He asks them to think of their younger brother or sister when they get into a vehicle, and if they won't buckle up for their own sakes, then they should buckle up for their loved ones, who really need and want them around. For more information about their wonderful foundation, go to www.AlexaHugs.com.

My Own Journey Through Grief

I'm not at liberty to share the details about what initiated the biggest grief process I've experienced in my life. It involved someone to whom I was very close to, whom I grew up with, and who, as an adult, tried to end his life three times within an 18-month period. I was there each time in the ICU, taking off work for weeks at a time, to hold his hand, sing old familiar songs to him, and tell him stories of our youth—about playing tag long after it got dark and sharing the most innocent, sacred parts of our childhood. I did all of this while he remained unconscious, kept alive only by tubes and machines that supplied him with food and breathed for him.

These events have had the deepest impact on my life (outside of giving birth to my two daughters). They made me reflect on who I truly was and what was most important to me. Through this tremendous grief, I was able to grow deeply and develop more fully into who I am today.

My friend survived his attempts, although he was forever changed. I grieved the loss of who he'd been in my life—a wonderful friend with whom I'd shared so much of my life and to whom I felt deeply connected. After his attempts he was heavily medicated and became a mere shell of the man (and boy) he once was. I lost the person I used to laugh with until my sides ached, and I lost one of my dearest friends with whom I had shared my deepest thoughts and dreams. He hadn't died, but the person he'd been, until that point, was gone.

In a moment of extraordinary clarity, I realized that a large part of my grief was the loss of his old personality. I missed the funny, wise, cool person he was on the outside. I liked how proud I felt with him because he was so charismatic, and everyone seemed to like him so easily. In this moment of clarity, I began to look deeper into who this kindhearted man was, beyond his external self. During all the time I spent with him after his attempts, I learned to see his inner self more clearly, beyond his personality, and to connect more deeply with the truth of who he was at a soul level. I discovered that it was his amazing essence, which neither time nor circumstances could change, that I most loved about him.

This experience helped me not only love others better but also myself in a new and beautiful way. I began to see others beyond their exteriors, past their behavior or words, and perceive what was shining from within. I became aware of a deeper truth: no matter who we are on the outside, we all have a beautiful soul within us.

The second gift that I received from this difficult experience was that I began to view and value my life in a whole new way. I wanted to live the dreams that I'd always had for myself, but that I'd somehow held myself back from. I clearly saw the fragility of life and that time wasn't something that we were necessarily guaranteed. I decided then to take the leap and start my own private practice— something I'd wanted to do since I left graduate school 14 years earlier. I'd been working for the elementary schools in Cheyenne for a decade and, although I loved the children, I knew I wasn't living my dream. I'd gone to graduate school with the dream of having my own private practice, and it was time to bring that dream into fruition.

Since 2007, I've been a private practice psychotherapist, and it's been the most rewarding work of my career so far. Out of so much grief came the courage to pursue what my heart had truly desired. My friendships and relationships are much deeper now, and I continue to make deeper, soul-level connections with the people who show up in my life.

In his book *Man's Search for Meaning*, psychiatrist and Holocaust survivor Viktor Frankl said,

> "What was really needed was a fundamental change in our attitude toward life. We had to learn ourselves, and furthermore, we had to teach the despairing men, that it did not really matter what we expected from life, but rather what life expected from us. We needed to stop asking about the meaning of life, and instead think of ourselves as those who were being questioned by life—daily and hourly."

When we accept that grief and suffering are a part of life and we find the meaning in that suffering, we're able to transcend it.

Healing through grief is possible. By allowing ourselves to be with our experience, we can transform the pain into something that can eventually become beautiful in our lives. Just as Rumi said in "The Guest House," sometimes grief "clears us out" for some new delight, unknown and often unseen to us at the time. The lives that are waiting for us on the other side can be illuminated, full of greater sparks than we ever imagined.

Healing Through Grief- Top 5 Takeaways

1. We have a natural tendency to avoid pain. It can be easy to avoid painful feelings as well but what we resist, persists. Just acknowledging the feeling and breathing into where you feel it in your body, can help it dissipate.

2. There is no order or time limit to how you experience your grief. It is your journey and it will not look like anyone else's. It is helpful to verbalize to others what you need from them so they can support you in the way that you truly need.

3. As Hafiz said, you can welcome all feelings that arrive into your life and know that each emotion that comes is important and may be something that is clearing you out for some new delight.

4. Out of the depth of our pain we can often find ways to reach out and actually help others through sharing our grief story or through sharing what was born within us during our grief journey that might speak to or inspire others.

5. Take time to be with your feelings and use it as a time to reflect on what is truly important in your life. It might just be the time you decide to take a risk and ignite the dreams you have always wanted to catch fire.

Chapter 6

Growing Grit and Resilience

"Resilience is not what happens to you. It's how you react

to, respond to,

and recover from what happens to you."

--Jeffrey Gitomer

In order to allow ourselves to ignite the sparks in our lives, we need to stoke our inner flame and cultivate a sense of grit and resilience. This is something that we can foster and grow within ourselves to helps us navigate through life's bumps and challenges.

I grew up thinking that grit and resilience were something people were born with—like the cowboys of the Old West that I'd see on TV. When I thought of "grit," I conjured up images of warriors or weathered sea captains. That was what it meant to be tough. Interestingly, as a child, all of the images in my mind were male.

The more life experience I had, however, the more I was able to understand that real grit and resilience were actually attributes that grew from facing, going through, and surviving hardships. I also learned that this was a quality in males and females alike.

My father grew up on the wheat fields of Nebraska and farmed alongside his father and brother until he left for college at the age of 18. My grandfather Ivan was of Danish descent, and we all called him "The Great Dane" because of his inner strength, incredible work ethic, and the fact that he was a tough old dog.

From the large kitchen window of their home, which was perched atop a rolling hill, one could literally see hundreds of acres of wheat land stretching out below. My father told me a story from his childhood that exemplified the inner resilience and grit my grandfather possessed.

My father remembers being about 10 years old and standing in the kitchen with my grandfather while they looked out of the kitchen window as dark, ominous clouds began to gather and billow across the sky. They watched as the clouds continued to roll in, building up until they released their fury on the crops below. My father and grandfather watched helplessly as golf ball–sized hail pulverized their crops and destroyed the all of the acres of wheat in one foul swoop.

He said my grandfather never got angry, or yelled, or cursed the sky. He merely put his arm around my father's shoulder, held him tight for a moment, and said, "There will be next year, my boy. There will be next year."

This story was powerful for me because my grandfather had just seen his crops—the main source of his family's income—absolutely destroyed, and he'd taken it all in stride. He had a deep faith that sustained him through times like these. He was a farmer who had worked the land his whole life and who knew the challenges and rewards, the rises and falls, the loss as well as the bountiful harvest of his hard work. He knew that in life there were indeed seasons. Some of reaping, some of sowing, and some of rebuilding. Through my grandfather's life experience of farming the land, he'd developed real grit and resilience to overcome life's challenges.

How do we grow this deep reservoir that can sustain us in difficult times? In my experience, the most important thing has been to hold to a morning ritual that I can count on to fortify me and bring me to center, no matter what the circumstances are in my life. Through repetition and consistency, I've created a solid foundation that supports me. When I feel as if I can't rely on anything else, I can rely on myself to show up in the morning, take the time to express my gratitude, write my affirmations, and listen to something positive that reminds me that I'm more than the present circumstances. When I do this, life shows up for me in a wonderful way. I've primed my mind and heart, and I've helped guide my perspective in a way that will be most beneficial to me as I start my day.

This practice helps builds resilience. We don't just have one new idea or change one thing about ourselves and say, "A-ha! I am now resilient!" It's a little-by-little, day-by-day practice that will keep us going when times get tough. All else may feel undone in your world, but having something you can return to, hold on to, and rely on will make whatever situation you face so much more bearable.

The Unsinkable Molly Bloom

I interviewed Molly Bloom on *The Spark*. Her story is amazing. In 1999, Molly was ranked third in the world in freestyle skiing. She suffered from chronic neck and back pain, which caused her to retire early from the sport. In lieu of going to law school, Molly decided to move to Los Angeles and live on a friend's couch for a while.

She started working for a man who ran an underground poker game. Eventually, she got involved in helping him run the game. Now, this wasn't just an ordinary poker game. The players were some of the most famous people in Hollywood, including major sports figures and rock stars. Ben Affleck, Leonardo DiCaprio, and Toby Maguire were regulars, just to name a few. When her boss wanted to take a part of her tips and quit paying her for the regular secretarial work, she did for him, Molly took over the game and ran it bigger and better herself.

As time went on, one of the players wanted a cut of her tips as well, and being a powerful man, when she refused to oblige, he cut Molly out of her own game. She went through huge feelings of betrayal and depression, but she was not to be defeated. Molly started a new game in New York City, where the buy-in to sit at the table was $250,000 a game.

Molly ran the most lavish poker games in the world with movie stars, athletes, royalty, and music stars as players. It wasn't uncommon for hands to go into the millions of dollars. The Russian mafia had players at the table, and the Italian mafia eventually wanted a cut of the money Molly was making. A horrible scene took place one night when one of them showed up at her apartment, beat her severely, robbed her, threatened her family, and stuck a gun in her mouth.

The biggest arrest of mobsters in New York City's history is probably what ended up saving Molly's life. The men who had threatened her never showed up again and most likely ended up in prison. When Molly's name came up in connection with the game, a federal indictment and her arrest by the FBI ended her career as a game runner. The FBI wanted her to reveal the names of all of the players and release the messages they had sent her. Although Molly would have faced 10 years in prison if she was convicted, due to her own personal integrity, she'd decided not to reveal the content of the messages that felt would ruin their lives and the lives of their families if released. She ended up not being convicted Molly stated, if she'd had to give up that information and ruin all of those live, then that would have been "the true-life sentence."

Molly underwent a powerful transformation when she quit running the game. She went to rehab to deal with her drug addiction, got clean and sober, and through meditation and continued involvement in 12-step groups she regained her life. In my interview with her, she shared that she's found what is truly meaningful to her: her family, her sobriety, and giving back in gratitude for all she's been given.

From her experience in the gambling world, Molly wrote the book *Molly's Game*, which caught the eye of director Aaron Sorkin. It was adapted into an Academy Award–nominated movie under the same name, starring Jessica Chastain as Molly. She's been living an amazing and inspirational life ever since. She now tours the US and Europe speaking about her experience and the deeper lessons she's learned.

As a young girl, she'd learned the skills of tenacity, dedication, and determination. This was evident in her success as a national champion freestyle skier. Molly used that same inner strength and tenacity to pull herself through the difficult times she faced both during and after her experience in the underground gambling world.

These days, Molly gets her joy from connection to family and friends and from giving back to the larger community. She started the nonprofit foundation Full Bloom where she wants to help create co-working spaces and networks for female entrepreneurs. Molly's found her own way to bloom again and to lead a more fulfilling, more meaningful life.

Reinventing herself through her most difficult times, Molly has developed a deep and beautiful sense of self, as well as true resilience and grit.

The Mindset of Resilience

There are certain ingredients that go into planting and cultivating a thriving garden. We have to take care of it, make sure it gets adequate water and sunlight, and pull the weeds.

Like a garden, resilience can be grown. It involves pulling the weeds of negative thoughts and planting the flowers of positive feelings by focusing on day-to-day positive experiences. As we tend to this inner garden, we begin to cultivate the inner calm, strength, and happiness that will allow us to bloom.

The more you practice ways to calm down your reactive minds, the more you will grow this kind of healthy, flourishing garden in your mind. One way too quiet your mind, is to find a quiet place where you can sit uninterrupted, even for 10 minutes. Begin by just focusing on your breathing and notice the physical sensation of breath going in and out of your body. Feel into your hands and notice the sensation there and then do the same with your feet. Bring your attention to your heart center. Imagine you are breathing in and out from this place. You might even say to yourself, "I breathe in love, I breathe out peace," as a kind of a mantra that will keep your thoughts occupied and allow you to begin to center yourself in a deeper way. Returning to this practice daily will help build that resilient inner core and give you a safe place you can return to no matter what is happening in your day.

You can build this inner garden in many ways. Mindfulness, gratitude, meditation, prayer, visualization, breathwork, relaxation, and cultivating awareness are all ways with which to change the way you think and feel. Chose the one(s) that work best for you. Through this daily practice, you will strengthen your resilience to deal with the challenges that arise in your life.

Getting Gritty

I've been through some extremely difficult times in my life. A single mom at age 22., not only did I finish my undergraduate degree, but lived on my own and put myself through graduate school. Living in a little apartment in downtown Denver, I was so strapped for money that after rent and all my bills were paid, we lived on $50 a week which was used to buy gas and groceries.

I took a year off from dating to just focus on my work and my daughter. These were mostly happy times. I had amazing girlfriends at work, loved my time with my daughter, and felt so proud of putting myself through grad school. During that time, some kind of deeper inner strength started to build inside of me. No one told me to go get my master's degree. I just knew I wanted to keep evolving professionally and knew the only way for me to get there was through furthering my education. So, I went for it.

There were also lonely times when I longed for another adult to share my life with. So, I read a lot, prayed a lot, journaled, and wrote poetry to help me through that period. I reached out to friends on the phone after my daughter was asleep and, once a month, went back up to Fort Collins to connect with my family.

Looking back on those times, I can see how strong and determined I was to improve my life and enrich my daughter's life. It took a lot of courage to move to the big city of Denver with her, not knowing a soul, and having to figure it all out on my own- from day care to grocery shopping and everything in between.

Those years and those experiences of being alone are what helped me develop grit. Knowing that I could make it on my own and still enjoy life despite the ups and downs gave me an inner strength that I've built on ever since.

Take inventory of the times you've grown grit in your life. As you reflect on the difficult times you've faced and overcome, look at the inner resources developed as a result of what you experienced. We rarely stop to look at what we've actually gained from our challenges. Often, we're just thankful we got through them. We're glad to get as far away from them as possible and see them as just images we choose to ignore in the rearview mirror on the road of life.

It's important to acknowledge the inner resources you see in yourself so you can build on them as well. Sometimes we use wit, humor, or our language skills to get us through. Sometimes, it's sheer determination and tenacity that helps us deal with life when times get tough. Whatever your strengths are, focus on them. Validate yourself for using them. And keep working to enhance your inner resources.

You may not realize you already have the inner resources to deal with whatever comes your way. The way you grow resilience and grit is also by realizing that these attributes are already there. You just need to tend to them. And as you focus on the strengths that are already there, through your attention you are fertilizing them and helping them to grow even stronger and take deeper root within you.

Over a decade ago, I was at a training with Dr. Dan Siegel, clinical professor of psychiatry at the UCLA School of Medicine and executive director of the Mindsight Institute. He taught me an invaluable tool called "The Wheel of Awareness," which has helped me navigate through rough waters in my own life and build a deeper sense of resilience. Just a couple of months ago, I had the honor of having Dan as a guest on *The Spark* and got to revisit the importance of this tool.

Through years of research, and now over 30,000 research participants, Dan has been able to prove the deep effectiveness of "The Wheel of Awareness," a model for growing resilience, calm, well-being, and connectedness. He said the model came from a round table in his office where he sat with students. It is a highly effective tool for building inner resources that will deeply serve your life.

"The Wheel of Awareness"

This mindfulness practice is one that you can do every morning for 20 minutes (or more, if you wish). It may also be helpful to record your own voice guiding you through the practice until you become familiar with it. You begin by imagining a wheel with a hub in the middle and four spokes that go out to the rim of the wheel. The hub represents the presence within us that notices our thoughts, feelings, and life experience.

When I'm doing this practice, I imagine that the hub is in my solar plexus. I think of this as the serene place within me from which I can notice whatever else is happening on the surface of my life. From my hub in my solar plexus, I visualize the wheel extending all the way around me, and, I notice the things that are happening on the rim of my experience.

Imagine that this wheel all around you is divided into four parts. The first part is your five senses. The second part is your interior sensing. The third part is your mental activities. And the fourth part is the sense of interconnectedness.

Close your eyes, take a deep breath into your belly and begin to relax the muscles of your body. Envision your hub at the center of your being and the rest of the wheel radiating out around you. Relax into this hub and take some deep breaths into this place. From here, send a spoke of attention to the first part of the wheel; your five senses.

One at a time, focus on each of your five senses for a few moments. Let yourself really experience each of them. Even with your eyes closed, you can notice patterns, colors, and the way the light filters in. Allow yourself to listen to sounds. Listen to the way they arise, come into awareness, and then fade away. Breathe in and notice the fragrances you become aware of. You may notice the smell of the air or of your own skin. Just notice. Allow yourself to explore the taste in your mouth. It may be something that you just ate or drank. Or the taste of your saliva. Feel your skin covering the entire exterior of your body. Notice how your clothes feel on your body. How your hair touches your face or skin. The sensation of jewelry or glasses you're wearing. See if you can feel a slight air current on your skin. Just notice all of these sensations. After you've explored all five senses, return your attention to your hub, and take a deep breath back into that place.

Then, send your second spoke of attention to the part of the wheel that represents interior sensing. Feel your body from the inside—one toe at a time, one foot at a time. Go up through each of the body parts and explore the sensation and aliveness in each one. Take your time and explore every muscle, bone, and internal organ. Just notice your inner experience. After exploring the entire interior of your body, return your attention back to the hub and breathe deeply.

Send the third spoke of attention to the part of the wheel that focuses on your mental activities—thoughts, emotions, and memories. I love this part. It's fascinating to become aware of how thoughts appear in your mind. Do they just seem to pop in to your mind, or do they seem to slide in from one side of your head or another? You can actually begin to count your thoughts as they appear. One important aspect of this part of the wheel is to experience your thoughts as if they were clouds in the sky. They appear and disappear; they float into awareness and then fade away. We don't have to define ourselves by our thoughts. They're just mental activities that are constantly happening regardless of whether we tune in to them or not. They're even happening when we're sleeping, which means they're not truly "us." After you explore your thoughts and the pictures and memories that are connected to them, return your attention to your hub.

After a few deep breaths, send the fourth spoke of attention to the last section of the wheel, where you can notice your connection to others. This can be a profound and powerful part of the experience. Begin with feeling your connection to the people you love very deeply. As you focus on this, imagine that you have rings of connection that radiate out from you, like concentric circles radiating out from a stone thrown into a pond. From here, allow that sense of connection to grow. Begin to notice your connection to acquaintances. Pause for a moment to really experience it. Allow the sense of connection to continue to expand to the people in your community. Some may be people whom you recognize, and some may be strangers. Continue to extend that sense of connection to people living in your state. Then, slowly extend that connection to your nation. Finally, extended that sense of connection into other countries— beyond the oceans into other continents—and allow it to encircle the entire world. Just notice the connection you have with all living things. Allow that sense of connection to return and reside in your own heart.

When you're ready, return your attention to your hub and rest in that awareness and feel into how good your entire being is feeling.

Dan Siegel has done this exercise with tens of thousands of people. The feedback he gets from individuals about their experience of exploring the hub of awareness is that they feel deeply tranquil. They also experience a sense of timelessness, a sense of oneness, and a sense of God (in whatever way that is defined for them).

This beautiful practice builds the inner resilience that takes us beyond life's circumstances. It helps us cultivate a sense of deep calm that becomes a reservoir to sustain us through life's most difficult challenges.

Growing resilience and grit are essential pieces for creating a spark-filled life. They allow our inner light to shine even through the darkest of times. They remind us that we have an inner flame that can't be extinguished. Through mindfulness and continued practice, they allow that flame to grow and to illuminate our lives.

Growing Grit and Resilience – Top 5 Takeaways

1. Just like a garden, grit and resiliency are something you can grow.

2. A daily ritual of prayer, mediation, or affirmation can help sustain you during challenging times. Knowing you have a foundation and daily practice you can return to provides a routine you can rely on to support you.

3. Like Molly Bloom, you can grow grit and resiliency when you listen to and follow your own truth. Acting out of your own integrity fortifies you and gives you the strength to deal with difficult situations.

4. Take inventory of your life and the challenges you have already overcome. As you take stock of these, write down the attributes you already possess and the grit you have already shown in your life. You are stronger and have more resources than you think!

5. You can utilize the wheel of awareness as a deep, transformational tool to grow a solid core and foundation of strength, resiliency, and inner peace in your life. Through daily practice you

can grow this inner core and know you have the
inner grit to deal with whatever comes your
way.

Chapter 7

Reinventing Your Life

"Your power to choose your direction of your life allows you to reinvent yourself, to change your future, and to powerfully influence the rest of creation."

—Stephen Covey

So, you've made it. You've come through some storms in your life to the other side, only to find out that you're feeling a little disoriented and not quite sure how this new chapter of your life will unfold or what this new reality will look like.

When you find yourself at this new and foreign place, it's essential that you begin to ground yourself in the present moment. Your brain loves familiarity. When things are unfamiliar, the brain goes on high alert scanning the unfamiliar environment for any kind of potential threat. This can raise your feelings of anxiety, especially if you start playing the "What If" game. This is the game your brain plays trying to predict the future and potential negative scenarios of what might happen. It is just your brain trying to keep you safe, but it is *not* helpful. After a major loss or a challenging chapter in your life, you can feel as if you've lost your internal compass. It can be difficult to just navigate through your day to day life, much less, venture into the unknown future that may look and feel very different after the loss.

As we learn how to practice being in the now, we're able to bring greater calm and peace into our lives. When we try to predict the future, we often feel anxious. When we continually fret about the past, which we have no power to change, we begin to feel helpless and depressed. Learning how to focus our thoughts and attention on the present moment can help soothe us into a more positive state of well-being. The point of power is in the present moment. From this place, we can begin to look at what truly lights us up—the spark filled path we'd like to pursue.

Focusing Your Attention on the Present

If I told you to bring your attention to the wall in front of you, and then to your feet, and then your lap, you'd be able to choose where you placed your attention. If you followed my directions, you'd be making the choice to place your attention on each of these places. Ironically, you'd also be making the choice *not* to focus on whatever it was you were thinking about beforehand. That's your point of power. You have the power to direct your attention wherever you choose, no matter what's going on outside or inside of you.

The point of entry into the present moment is making the choice to be here, now. It's reigning in our thoughts and letting go of the pull to obsess on the past or worry about what the future may hold.

If you've ever watched a news station where they have that tickertape of news events running at the bottom of the screen, you have an idea of how thoughts stream on the screen of the mind. At any time, you can choose to pay attention to one of the news items running by on the tickertape. This story then becomes your "primary news" and what you focus on in your mind.

As I mentioned before, you're constantly thinking—even when you're not consciously aware of it or when you're sleeping. 95% of our thoughts are subconscious. In waking states, you might pluck something out of the stream of thoughts in your mind and allow it to be full screen. It might be a thought that leads to negative feelings of worry, regret, or doubt. What's amazing is that once you become aware that the thought is just one of the hundreds of thousands of thoughts that are constantly running in your mind, you can choose *not* to focus on it as well. If the thought you plucked out doesn't serve you, you can choose to return it to the stream of thoughts and pick up a different one that serves you better.

When you're in the present moment, you're better able to observe these thoughts as they run across the screen of your mind and choose the thoughts that serve you. From that place, you can start to enjoy the good feelings that are naturally connected to more positive thoughts.

Letting Go of Labels

A big part of igniting your best life is letting go of the labels you, or someone else may have put on you, so can be more authentically you in the present moment. As a child, before you become socially conditioned, you had a free, untamed spirit inside of you that was not afraid to express itself. In his book *The Four Agreements*, Don Miguel Ruiz speaks about what happens to this wild spirit as you grow up: "After years and years of trying to please other people's images of what you should be, after trying to find out who you really are, you finally give up and accept other people's images of what you are. But there is something inside you that longs to be free; it is always telling you, 'This is not who I really am. This is not what I really want.'"

So, we become domesticated. Little boys are taught that the only acceptable emotions for men are happiness or anger. Tears aren't tough. Only sissies cry. Men should be serious, not emotional. They are aggressive and competitive. A real man should be economically powerful and socially successful. For men in our society, success is often defined by money and power, not the content of their heart. Even though we may feel we're living in an enlightened era, so many of those stereotypical norms still survive, and they help dictate how little boys are conditioned to see themselves and influences their self-worth as adults.

When I work with men in my practice, we often talk about the incredible—and often, difficult—18-inch journey from their head to their heart. Men are problem solvers, and it's easy for them to hide in their rational mind. This can be great protection from having to feel the more complicated dealings of the heart. When men find this deeper inner voice, it is a beautiful thing to witness it emerging. It takes true courage to look at what dwells there. And it takes tremendous strength to let go of the ego and be vulnerable. I've found that when men have explored this vulnerable place, they're able to let go of archaic stereotypes of what it means to be a man, heal old hurts, and live a far more connected and fulfilling life with access to a full range of emotions. Life just becomes a richer experience. Men and women truly do experience similar emotions and being able to articulate their emotional experience is a healing, transformative, and helps create connections to others in deep and meaningful ways.

For women, often times their sense of value is still strongly tied to looking young and beautiful and less on their intelligence and who they are inside. There are still unspoken rules and stereotypes about how females should behave, as well. Even though it is archaic, little girls often get the message they should be seen and not heard, should be smart but not too smart, should always be nice, and put others needs before their own. Expressing anger, even appropriately, and standing up for themselves, females often run the risk of being labeled a "bitch." Women can lose their voice by trying to fit these stereotypes and please others before looking inwardly and truly serving their own souls.

I had a female client who came to me a year ago broken spirited, self-worth completely diminished, and physically suffering from many ailments after leaving a 43-year abusive relationship. At 63 she had lost her energy, her happiness, and at times, even her will to live. Her ex-husband had called her so many names throughout the years, that she had internalized them, and those labels had become her identity. Through weekly therapy (and sometimes twice a week when things were tough) she began to find that inner voice. She quit putting all of her children and grandchildren's needs before hers. She learned what lit her up inside and how to plug into a life that was creative, meaningful, and fulfilling. Most importantly for her, she learned to have boundaries with others, reclaim her voice, and had the deep awareness that she was the one who got to dictate who she was and no longer let anyone else define that for her. When she walked into my office for a visit last week after not seeing each other for a while, she looked radiant, healthy, and full of life. Three months ago, she started a blog, Kaleidoscope Strong and it is helping other abused women to find their voices and empower them to leave abusive relationships and learn how to truly thrive in the world.

To live a spark-filled life, you have to break free from societal stereotypes and cultural conditioning. You can no longer define yourself by any negative label your past self or someone else has put on you. You can do this by finding your own inner voice and then expressing that more authentic self to the world. It starts by claiming what your own truth really is. This is a task that can be daunting if we've mainly defined ourselves by the expectations of others. But it can be done. There are many things you can do to help that healing begin and reclaim the real you.

The Empty Chair Technique

Some of my female clients have expressed that they don't even know how to find this voice because it's been stifled for so long. The empty chair technique can be an amazingly powerful tool to help men or women find their voice and regain their confidence in speaking up for themselves.

To begin with, I invite my clients to write out what they would like to say to the person they feel they've lost their voice to. Sometimes, we write this out together. It can be helpful to practice deep breathing, relaxation, and visualization to help get in touch with your heart space in order to find this voice. I encourage my clients to float back to an earlier version of themselves that felt more authentic so they can write without any filters, straight from the heart. After my clients feel they've written what they truly want to say, I invite them to imagine that the person they wish they could talk to is sitting in the empty chair in my office. By speaking out loud what their hearts have most wanted to say, there is a sense of empowerment that comes from just speaking their truth and the healing process of reclaiming their voice truly begins.

Whether you're male or female, this activity can be wonderfully helpful. Hearing yourself speaking the words out loud also gives you a chance to reevaluate your message and whether you would want to say things differently. Even if you never choose to have this conversation in real life, practicing speaking your truth out loud helps you to define it. This exercise can give you the confidence to finally talk with the person with whom you need to have a conversation. And real success isn't necessarily determined by the outcome of the conversation. It's in your ability to find and express your true voice and authentic self.

Keep Shining Your Light

In 2017, I traveled to Cabo San Lucas, where I had an amazing experience swimming with the dolphins, watching grey whales, and paddle boarding in the Sea of Cortez. It was a dream vacation with my husband and good friends. Nights were filled with great conversation and lots of laughter. At dinner on the last night, one of the men from our group stated that a couple of the women, including me, were laughing too loud. He also made shaming comments to us about our voices being too loud.

It triggered a huge reaction in me, igniting an intensity that I felt had to be expressed. I spoke to him first individually about how hurtful his words and behavior had been, and he ended up apologizing. He was embarrassed, and he realized it was his own inability to just cut loose and have fun that had led to the comment.

I appreciated the conversation and his apology. But I wanted to share the message that it's often other people's inability to deal with their own suppressed feelings that makes it difficult for them to deal with others' joy. I wanted to encourage and inspire women to give themselves permission to be their authentic selves and not allow others to dampen their exuberance. The next day, I wrote this post on Facebook (which ended up being one of the most responded-to posts I've ever had).

March 8, 2017

Recently, I was told by someone that I have a loud voice and that I laugh too loud. I'm sorry if my joy and my exuberance for life makes you feel uncomfortable or puts you in touch with your own lack of authenticity.

I am not rude or obnoxious with my voice, nor have I been a person who yells at others. But I will not live my life in a "polite" little box or minimize my vibrancy because women are meant to be seen and not heard.

I will not dim the shine on my soul that finds expression in this word so I can fit into someone else's mold of what it means to be a lady.

I will not be silenced or shushed because you cannot tolerate the unexpressed vibrancy in yourself.

I will continue to shine, express, exude, emit, emanate, radiate, and experience my joyful spirit manifest in this world.

I will continue to bring all the kindness, love, and healing to this world I can possibly muster.

I will continue to be unapologetically myself.

Life wasn't meant to be lived in muted tones at volume two.
Life is meant to be lived out loud.

Crank. It. Up.

Your voice matters. How you see yourself and how you express yourself in this world matters. Don't let anyone dim your shine.

Reclaiming Ourselves

In July of this 2018, I attended Marianne Williamson's two-day workshop, Powerful Beyond Measure, in Denver. It was life transforming in many ways, and it took my awareness of self and of spirit working in my life to the next level. Although I already felt in touch with "my voice," I was able to step out of my ego and drop into my heart in a deeper way than I've ever experienced.

Marianne's message was a call to action to get centered, invite spirit to work in our lives, and bring love and our voices together for the common good of humankind and our planet.

Love is the source of salvation for our planet—and for us. Marianne stressed that when we choose love over fear, we can become a force for change, and we can create miracles both in our everyday lives and in the lives of others. As we realize our connection to spirit and each other, we can become a voice for creating positive change in our world, redefine what's important to us, and create a life that's fulfilling to us in greater ways than we ever imagined.

I've been reading Marianne's work for over 20 years. Her voice is one that has guided me through difficult times and helped me experience my life in a deeper and more meaningful way. Meeting her and talking with her after the workshop was a great joy for me. As I walked up to her, she looked into my eyes and asked, "Have we met before?" I said, "I am sure we have in spirit." I was so thankful for our conversation and our connection that it led to her agreeing to be a guest on my show—which was not only a blessing but a miracle for me because before speaking with her, I'd been a bit hesitant to invite her. But when I made the choice to just go beyond my fear and ask her, she very graciously accepted and said that she would love to do the interview. Finding your voice is indeed a powerful force that can lead to amazing things.

Beyond Voice

Aside from the importance of finding our voice, we also have to start taking inventory of what creates sparks in our lives. In my radio interview with my dear friend and clinical psychologist Larry Bloom, we talked about the importance of how to craft an ideal life after major transitions and how to redefine ourselves.

Larry spoke about the importance of taking stock things we've really wanted to do but have never tried. The essential element is to step out of fear and take action. For him, it was playing the blues harmonica. He took lessons for six months before humbly admitting that maybe blues harmonica wasn't his thing. Larry made an effort and dove into a new endeavor that lit him up. In the end, whether he was good at it or not didn't matter. What was important is that he fully pursued something he truly enjoyed. In doing so, he added a positive and enjoyable new dimension to his life.

That's the problem. We get too serious about starting a new hobby or doing something we've never done before. Just try it. It may be art or music, dancing or singing, or joining a hiking group. It could be learning how to paddle board or joining a writing group or a book club. Anything that takes you out of your regular experience and allows you to experience a more expanded version of you.

I've known Larry since I was 13 years old, and he's been instrumental in helping me see myself more clearly, believe in myself in deeper ways, and helped me to define and go after my dreams. It was our conversation in his office at Colorado State University, back in 1986, that changed the direction of my life. I'd been struggling with what to do about college after deciding not to return to art school. During that conversation, Larry said to me, "Stephanie, you are a natural at this. If you want to go into counseling, I know the advisor in the social work department. Go talk to her." And so, I did. That conversation led to what has now been a 30-year career and the most fulfilling work I could have ever imagined.

For years, Larry also encouraged me to get into radio. He had always told me what a great voice I had and that I would be awesome on the air. He helped me see that I had a certain charisma and natural gift of connecting with others, which helped me to cultivate the ability to truly see myself as a radio talent. When my producer first approached me about doing my own radio show, this belief about myself and my ability to do radio was already instilled in me. He said I practically jumped out of my seat, when he asked, clapping my hands with a confident, "YES!"

For the first episode broadcast of The Spark with Stephanie James, Larry was the natural choice as my first guest. He's been one of my guides to living a fulfilling, ignited life, and he's been my North Star many times as I've navigated the unknown waters of this human experience. I'm deeply grateful for his mentorship. To this day, Larry still encourages me to expand beyond whatever limiting thoughts might be holding me back. Tucked in the back of my head, his voice is still chanting, "You. Can. Do It!"

It doesn't matter so much *what* you do—just that you do *something*. Write down a list of things you enjoy or things you used to enjoy when you were a kid. Get in touch with your playful nature. See what would add more spark to your life—and plug in to that. What's wonderful is that if it doesn't end up being a good fit for you (like Larry and the blues harmonica), you can go on to do something else that brings you even more joy and fulfillment.

Whether it's fly-fishing or salsa dancing, let your heart be your guide and check your ego at the door. We all have a desire to have novelty in our lives. The beautiful thing is that we have the power to create it. We just have to make the choice.

If it feels as though your own fears, negative thoughts, or limiting beliefs are keeping you from creating a more spark-filled life, find a mentor or a friend who has done the things you want to accomplish and/or who can help inspire you to ignite your life. You'd be surprised how many people are willing to share their wisdom, ideas, and experience to help you on the path to manifesting your greatest life. Reach out. Having a cheerleader on your sideline can help you move mountains and develop the many gifts you already have inside of you.

Another thing that can be helpful is to do a journaling exercise about how you'd like to see yourself a year from now. Include everything you can think of about your ideal life, and write it in only positive language using the present tense, as if it's already happening. Read this list out loud daily. As you begin to envision it every day, you'll be training your RAS to notice all the things that begin to show up that are leading you to having the life you're imagining. Hearing your own voice claiming this life is a powerful process indeed.

Finding Some of My Own Sparks

When I was 44 years old, I started singing with a modern folk band. We had fantastic professional musicians who were all extremely talented and creative and passionate about music. It just so happened that all of the musicians were also young males in their mid-20s. My friend Carol Anne, who also sang with the band, was my age, so we appropriately named the band Mrs. Robinson. It was an incredible and rewarding experience in many ways. We practiced six hours a week, and eventually, when we'd worked up 26 songs, we got a weekly gig at a local bar.

I took guitar lessons and started playing backup guitar and even lead guitar on a few songs. We did a digital recording of one of our shows, and I was able to joyfully share that CD with many of my friends and family members. It was an amazingly enriching, exciting, and expansive experience. I'll never forget the growth that happened throughout that process, and I'll always treasure that time as a catalyst that moved me to a new (and better) place in my life.

Although we were only together a couple of years, I'm so thankful for the experience. I learned a lot about myself and what gave my life meaning. I felt more alive during that time than I had in several years. It lit me up from the inside, and I radiated that light through every practice and performance.

Mid-Life Crisis

For as long as I can remember, if someone between the ages of 40 and 55 bought a new house, got divorce, changed careers, or bought a fancy new sports car, it was said, "Well, they're probably just going through a mid-life crisis." But as humans, changing things up and reevaluating our lives at that point is absolutely normal, natural, and part of our journey as we continue to find what is meaningful in our lives.

I prefer to call in a "mid-life transition" or "mid-life reinvention" because there actually doesn't have to be any "crisis" about it. It's during this time that we can become disillusioned with what we thought would bring us happiness in our lives: a career, a relationship, or material possessions. It's often the case that when we hit our mid-40s, we begin to reevaluate who we are, what creates true meaning for us, and how we want to live the next chapters of our lives.

In their 40s and 50s, some people notice their health has started to decline, or they aren't as active as they once were. Others notice that their entire life has been built around their kids. Now that their children are in high school or are no longer living at home, they become aware they don't have an identity outside of being parents, and they experience an emptiness when that role isn't as necessary as it once had been. Often times people begin to deepen their sense of spirituality and connection to a higher power as they are looking for true meaning in life. This can be a time to really tap into an expanded sense of their humanity and connection to something bigger than themselves. Some people become aware they have been only driven by their careers and find themselves truly desiring connection and a relationship or decide they are sick of traveling 3 out of 4 weeks during the month and want more of a sense of being grounded at home. "Been there, done that, don't really want to do it anymore," is what this stage can feel like.

When we reach this stage of life, we don't need to assume a whole new identity or leave our relationship of 20 years or buy a brand-new BMW. Not that any of those things are necessarily bad. In and of themselves, they're just not going to fulfill us. In the end, true meaning or fulfillment doesn't come from external things or circumstances. This is an inside job.

When we allow ourselves to reevaluate what's most important to us, where our passion lies, and what lights us up, we can begin to find the breadcrumbs that will lead us out of the woods and onto the path toward a more fulling life. During these times, we can shrug off old preconceived notions of what we "should" be doing and listen to our higher self for guidance. This is the time when we need to shrug off everyone else's opinion of us and what we're doing, we need to decide that we're going to stick to our own path, even if what that road is or where it's leading isn't clear yet (to others or ourselves.)

Through moments of quiet meditation, journaling, or working on clarifying goals by yourself—or in working with a life coach or therapist—you can navigate this transition beautifully. You have the power to define *your* life as *you* best see fit. Give yourself permission to listen to your highest calling—and answer it.

This next stage is uniquely yours. You get to design it. Take a few moments and allow yourself to think big. What do you want your life to look like? Write it down, in positive, present-tense language and read it out loud to yourself every day. Help yourself to envision and then create the life you truly desire. What you focus on, and what you speak out loud becomes like your prayer to the universe and amazing and wonderful things will begin to manifest in your life.

Reinvention in Action

Two amazing clients come to mind as I think of the art of reinvention. The first one is Sarah, a lovely 34-year-old woman. She was married to a man who had been diagnosed as bipolar but who refused to be medicated or get counseling to deal with his illness. Instead, he chose to self-medicate with pot and alcohol. The result was that his behavior was very erratic at times. He had explosive episodes during which he would scream, throw things, and basically, terrorize Sarah.

Sarah couldn't imagine herself leaving the marriage after being with this man for 14 years. She felt that she was his caretaker and that if she didn't love him, maybe no one would. Sarah had carried this burden for years and when she came to see me, she was very depressed, very anxious and very, very stuck.

Despite Sarah's repeated begging, her husband refused to join her in counseling, and his negative behaviors began to escalate. He wouldn't come home some nights, chose to hang out with his friends over her, and treated Sarah with great disrespect. She was desperate to find her own voice and get untangled from a very unhealthy relationship. She needed to focus on being responsible for her own life, and not for her husband's anymore. He had his own friends and family who supported him. By her own definition, Sarah's life had become very small as she tried to deal with the emotional rollercoaster of being with him and their volatile relationship.

In therapy, Sarah and I did a powerful three-year visualization into the future. It started with a relaxation exercise. Then, through a guided visualization process, Sarah met herself three years into the future, where she was able to ask her more evolved self a series of high-quality questions (such as what risks to take, whom to forgive, what the positive qualities of her future self were). The answers her "higher self" gave her helped guide the present time Sarah toward a greater future. Through an automatic writing process in the middle of the visualization, Sarah answered her 12 questions with the first thing that popped into her mind.

When we finished the visualization, Sarah had a roadmap into her future with guidance from her greater self, and she was able to access her deeper intuition. She had what she needed to build her new life.

Six months later, Sarah was happily single. She'd quit her low paying job, and she'd applied and been hired at a dream job on the coast of California. She was able to detach from her husband in a respectful and healthy way and reclaim her inner and outer life—experiencing new friends, new places, new activities (hiking and mountain biking). She was living a life that she'd never believed was possible.

I still stay in touch with her. Her life has continued to blossom and grow. She's now in a wonderful, healthy relationship (the two of them mountain biked together across the Southern states of North America) and Sarah continues to reinvent her life in amazing and powerful ways. When I spoke to her a few months ago on the phone, her laughter was contagious, and her vibrancy was palpable. She is in a job working for the forest service that she loves, she lives with the love of her life, and she is plugged into herself and activities that bring her true joy.

Sarah's clear vision enabled her to create a life that she absolutely loves.

Dean's story is another wonderful example of a mid-life transformation. Dean was a brilliant client I worked with several years ago. At 51 years of age, he'd moved up the corporate ladder and had achieved huge success. He'd pushed himself through school and, after receiving his PhD, continued to progress to higher positions in his field and more financial gain. Dean was the top man in his organization, a published author, and a global expert in his field. The only problem was that Dean was miserable.

When he came to see me, Dean said, "I feel like I have done all of the things that my parents expected of me and that other people have held as standards of what success means. I can't remember the last time I enjoyed my work. My marriage is suffering, I am suffering, and I feel like a foreigner in my own skin. I feel like I am living someone else's life."

One of the first things Dean and I worked on was this 18-inch journey from his head down into his heart. Because Dean was so brilliant, he lived mostly in his mind. He also resided there because life was easier to deal with from a rational and intellectual place rather than the emotional and messy place of his heart. It had never felt comfortable to him to delve into his feelings, so his career, constant travel, and writing had served him well. Until it didn't.

After three marriages, two of which didn't end well, he kept his emotions even more boxed up. He loved his current wife dearly, but he didn't know how to verbalize it to her, and he rarely allow himself to access those deeper feelings. He just "knew" he felt that way and expected her to just "know" he felt that way too.

So, we began with body mediations. I had him place his hand on his heart and focus on bringing his attention to that part of his body. At first, this was very uncomfortable for him, but eventually, it became easier and easier. We would just do this for five to 10 minutes each session—just focusing on breathing and gradually learning to reside in his heart.

We worked on self-compassion, exploring his wounded feelings as a little boy in boarding school. He'd been horribly teased, and he'd felt very different from the other boys. In order to survive his situation, he began to shut down his feelings. Dean and I also did several sessions of EMDR to help him reprocess these early traumatic events that had left him believing he wasn't good enough and that had created the beliefs that were now limiting him from living a fulfilling life.

As Dean began to access his heart, something wonderful happened. He started to see that he could no longer live the way he'd been living. He realized that he'd become a "Yes man" at work, and he no longer enjoyed the roles he played in his corporation. As his heart thawed out, he was able to see what his true passions were. He decided that he no longer wanted to be the committee chair on his board. Instead, he decided to pursue his individual contracts, which is where he felt he could really serve and connect with other people.

Dean also made a huge change by limiting the amount of travel he did for work, which enabled him to spend more time with his wife enhancing their relationship. He began to work on more effective communication with her, and he had weekly goals of demonstrating and verbalizing his love and appreciation. His whole definition of success was completely transformed.

As Dean reinvented this new life for himself, he found more fulfillment than he'd ever experienced or thought possible. He let go of his preconceptions of what happiness and success looked like. He discovered that, without love and deeper connection, exterior things ultimately left him feeling unfulfilled, lonely, and emotionally empty—even at the top of his career.

He and his wife began finding time to go bike riding, attend concerts, and garden together. Dean found extreme pleasure in being able to focus on their pets and build a guest cottage in the back yard. He reconnected with his family in a whole new way. Dean ignited his own life.

Sometimes, to reinvent ourselves and create our greatest lives, we have to think out of the box. Dean's box was the limiting beliefs he'd placed on himself about who he was and what he "had" to do to be a success. By living more fully in and from his heart, he was able to discover what he really wanted and create a beautiful reality. Operating from that place enhanced not only his life but the lives of the many others he was connected to as well.

You don't have to wait for a mid-life transition to reevaluate your life and start living from a more authentic place. It's never too late to reinvent yourself. This can be a constant renewal process that enables you to keep tuning into what really feeds your soul and keep creating the life of your dreams. Every six months you can look at the different areas of your life and determine what is serving you, what you need to let go of, and what might bring new energy into your life that you want to plug into.

When you discover the sparks that ignite your life and you find your true inner voice, you can live the life that you've always dreamed of. The power to create this life is within you.

Reinventing Your Life- Top 5 Takeaways

1. Focus your attention on the present moment so you can envision, create, and choose the life you want to create from yourself from a place that is not held captive of the past or fearful of the future. The present moment is your point of power.

2. Let go of labels of yourself (whether from someone else or self-inflicted.) You can begin to reclaim your voice through practicing The Empty Chair Technique and speaking your truth out loud.

3. Try new things. Be open to experience new things that might light you up in new ways. You don't have to do anything perfectly- just allow yourself to explore new activities and experience and just have fun with it!

4. You can reinvent yourself at any age. Take time to write down, meditate on, and then start plugging into what you want to experience in your life. You can design the life you truly want to live and then start living it by doing the things that bring you the most joy and meaning to your life.

5. Move into your heart space and evaluate what is meaningful and what you'd like to change about how you are living and being in the world. From this place you can begin to live a more authentic life that will ignite your heart and soul.

Chapter 8

Cultivating Joy

"Joy is what happens to us when we allow ourselves

to recognize how good things really are."

—Marianne Williamson

Nothing is more fulfilling in life than the experience of joy. I've heard it said that happiness is an emotion, but that joy is a spiritual experience. Cultivating joy is an essential piece of the life we truly want to create.

Martin Seligman is a psychologist and professor at Pennsylvania State University. In 1998, he was elected president of the American Psychological Association, and he helped bring positive psychology into popularity. Martin developed a psychology that focuses on an individual's character strengths and virtues as a positive counterpart to the *Diagnostic and Statistical Manual* (*DSM*), used by clinicians to diagnose patients, which focuses on negative symptoms and what could go wrong with an individual. For many years, I've used a couple of his clinically proven exercises, both with individuals and in my workshops, to help promote and extend feelings of joy.

The first exercise is one that Martin refers to as a "Joy Booster." It involves writing a letter of gratitude to someone who has positively and profoundly affected your life. The biggest component isn't just to write the letter or send it, but to personally deliver it and *read* it to the recipient. Based on Martin's research, the experience of seeing that person's positive response to you reading the letter to them, will give you a joy boost for up to three months.

The second exercise actually boosts your joy and sustains it for as long as you continue to do the exercise. By merely writing down and feeling into three things that you're most grateful for each morning, you begin to change the way you feel and bring more joy into your life. In a five-year longitudinal study, research subjects who continued to write in their gratitude journals had significant overall higher scores of joy (sustained throughout the five years) than those subjects who didn't.

Growing Joy

Many people are on a quest for happiness. Often, they pursue it through money, sex, drugs, possessions, and relationships. The problem with this kind of happiness is that it's always fleeting. Even after they've obtained the things they thought would bring them happiness or joy, they find they're not able to sustain that feeling, and they're left hungering for the next thing to fill that empty place.

One of the things that I use as a daily practice (and that has worked for many of my clients) is to feel joy as I begin my day. By identifying things that have brought me joy in the past, making the memory as vivid as possible, and allowing myself to marinate in those good feelings for a few moments helps the experience of joy grow inside me.

Remember, the mind has no concept of time. Whatever image you give it, the mind experiences it as happening now. That's why when you hold up a sad experience from the past, you can feel the feelings of sadness in that moment. It's also why you can think about something that you're afraid will happen in the future and feel the feelings of worry and anxiety in present time, even though it is not happening "now."

The wonderful thing about this exercise is that you can *choose* to feel and cultivate joy in this moment—no matter what your current circumstances may be.

In his book *Man's Search for Meaning*, Viktor Frankl said, "Everything can be taken from a man but one thing: the last of the human freedoms—to choose one's attitude in any given set of circumstances, to choose one's own way." This powerful statement helps us see that we can choose our attitude, and cultivate our own emotional experience, no matter what difficulties or challenges we face. It's within us. And it's up to us to tap into and develop our own experience of joy.

Pursuing Peace

Happiness is an emotion, and it comes and goes depending on the circumstance. But peace is a state of being. If we choose peace as the goal, not happiness, we make it possible for joy to grow inside of us and take root.

Learning to calm our minds is a wonderful way to cultivate peace. Our minds are like a frolicking puppy running at full speed, with ears flapping, tongue hanging out, and tail wagging. The mind is a busy, busy place. When we begin to quiet our mind, our judging mind that is always trying to determine if something is good or bad for us will naturally begin to "frolic." Our minds also have a difficult time staying in the moment because we are programmed to think our joy or happiness is outside of us. If we just looked the right way, had the right job, or improved our life in some way, then we could be happy and be at peace. We don't have to earn anything or be anything to find this sense of peace. Our work is to teach the puppy to sit and stay. We don't have to beat it into submission. We can train it with gentleness.

I suggest starting with five minutes of silence. Set an alarm and then just breathe slowly into your heart center. Focus on the pleasant sensations of your breath as you slowly inhale. Then, focus on the feelings of release and relaxation as you exhale. At the end of the five minutes, put a hand on your heart and focus on bringing in the feeling of joy either through a memory or because you get to experience a moment of peace.

Author and motivational presenter Brendon Burchard has a tool he uses for triggering his experiences of joy. In an interview with Lewis Howes, he talks about how he uses doorways as reminders to increase his joy. As he walks

through a doorway, he says to himself, "Bring the joy!"
This enhances his experience of joy throughout the day.
Through regular practice of "bringing the joy," he's
cultivated a mindset that enhances his life in a powerful
way.

Making Joy a Focus

In 2014, I was in a women's group that met monthly to
discuss individual goals and help each other grow. One of
the wonderful women in the group was a CPA who felt that
she didn't have a lot of joy in either her work or her
personal life. In one of the meetings, she decided that her
yearly goal was to have 365 days of joy. Realistically, she
knew that not every day would be totally joyful, but she
really wanted to expand feeling joy in her life. She began a
joy journal. At the end of each day, she wrote down all of
the things that had brought her joy that day.

By the time she'd written in her journal for 90 consecutive
days, she reported that, in addition to having more joy in
her life, she was more present to the joy *as it was
happening*. Because she'd trained her heart and mind to be
aware of joy, she was experiencing it in a much deeper and
more profound way.

Making Joy Stick

In Rick Hanson's book *Resilient: How to Grow an Unshakable Core of Calm, Strength, and Happiness*, he writes about how we can cultivate joy by noticing it as it shows up in our everyday life. Rick talks about how negative experiences are like Velcro in the brain because the brain is hardwired to keep us safe, whereas positive experiences slide off like Teflon.

Rick says if you just take a few breaths when something positive happens to you and pause for a moment—maybe putting your hand on your heart as you inhale—you'll send the message (along with some dopamine) to your brain that this is something valuable, which will help it stick in your memory. What you focus on really does expand. You'll begin to notice more and more of the things that make you feel good. It's powerful when you realize you can direct your attention to what you really want more of in your life.

I can imagine what you're thinking. "What about when we don't have joyful experiences, and it's really difficult to feel joy?" Sometimes, we don't. And sometimes, it really is hard to feel that way. The goal isn't to pretend that life isn't challenging. It's to be aware that we can choose joy and that we can enhance that feeling whenever you want to, no matter what circumstances we face.

When my outer reality isn't inspiring joy, or I've just had a hard day, I have a reservoir of joyful memories I can tap into to make the shift to a better place. Simply remembering my cousin Danelle's wedding reception—the feeling of being surrounded so many family members whom I love deeply and being out on the dance floor with my grandpa Oscar who was dancing a jig, can instantly put a smile on my face. The joy of that event was intoxicating. I think of the eight -hour drive I took yearly for 12 years with my daughters, Hailey and Acacia, and my stepdaughter, Kala, to go camping at Wiggins Fork in Wyoming. There was never a dull moment in that car. We cranked up the music, sang at the top of our lungs, laughed, told stories, and had a blast together. Just the thought of hugging my grandsons, August and Gunnard (who, I'm pretty sure, are the best huggers in the whole wide world), and listening to them laugh when I tickle them or sing them a funny song—bring a smile to my heart every single time. I can pull myself out of worry and get back into alignment with my joy when I tap into this reservoir of memory.

Think of your most joyful memories. As you practice remembering and feeling them, the joy will become more and more accessible to you when you need it. Write them down, if that's helpful. This isn't about ignoring reality. It's about making a conscious choice to experience joy. If you're going through a difficult experience, you can acknowledge whatever it is you're feeling, decide how long you want to feel that way, and then choose to experience a different emotion. As the late, great Joseph Campbell said, "Find a place inside where there's joy, and the joy will burn out the pain."

Robert Holden, Ph.D. author of *Happiness Now* and *Shift Happens*, writes, "What you focus on becomes familiar and what is familiar feels real to you." We can choose to feel good and focus on the memories and experiences that bring us true joy.

Places to Avoid: The Waiting Place

Oh, the Places You'll Go! by Dr. Seuss is a timeless book about the realities of life. It teaches that we're limitless, that we're full of potential, and that we can do anything we set our minds to—except for when we get stuck. It gives such a perfect description of how we can "soar to high heights" and how there will also be times when we'll feel lost and alone—when we'll encounter challenges no matter what path we choose.

Dr. Seuss says The Waiting Place is the most useless place...for people just waiting. People here are "waiting around for the snow to snow or waiting around for a Yes or No...or waiting, perhaps, for their Uncle Jake or a pot to boil, or a Better Break...Everyone is just waiting." In the illustrations, everyone is standing around in lines, expressionless. All movement forward has ceased.

The most painful Waiting Place, in my opinion, is one that we create when we're compromising our sense of self by wanting someone or something outside of ourselves to validate who we are. In my work with many single individuals, I often hear what happens when someone first meets a potential love interest. All of the sudden, a person who was a complete stranger only a day before, suddenly becomes the dictator of this individual's self-worth.

I often hear of the agony a person goes through waiting to see if the person they went on a date with contacts them again and it can become a huge inner yardstick with which they measure their sense of self, and self-worth. Anxious thoughts ransack their minds while they're in this Waiting

Place—waiting to see if they're worthy of further contact and connection.

This Waiting Place can also take the form of the "What If" game. In this game, we project all of our worries into the future and predict the worst outcomes. It's pretty hard to feel any joy when we're focused on all of the catastrophes that lie waiting for us. Waiting for test results. Waiting for information from a friend or loved one. It can become an endless loop of worry and anxiety.

When we project our worries into the future, there's no room for joy in the present. It doesn't serve you to worry about the future. It won't affect the outcome of the test (or any other circumstance). If you can bring yourself to the present moment and focus on centering, relaxing, and creating a sense of peace within yourself, you'll be much better able to deal with whatever lies ahead than if you're stressed and worried. If the worst really does happen, you'll be dealing with it on an empty tank instead of with a full reservoir of calm. Until you have that future information, be in the now. Focus on replenishing yourself at a deeper level so that you're better ready for whatever the future holds.

This will help you get out of the Waiting Place. You can move from feeling helpless and out of control to dealing with whatever is at hand in a calmer and more centered way. When you find yourself in a situation where you become aware you're placing your sense of joy in something outside of you, you can leave the Waiting Place and bring yourself back to center by asking yourself, "What power am I giving this situation over my thoughts and feelings?" We give our power away to others when we allow them to dictate how we feel about ourselves or determine the amount of joy we let in.

Unfortunately, the Waiting Place is where we delay our happiness. In our world of instant gratification, of iPhones, and the internet, any waiting can seem torturous. There's great value in cultivating patience. Being in the Waiting Place is denying ourselves joy by placing it outside of ourselves. We tell ourselves when we get the job, or the relationship, or have a better body, then we will allow ourselves to feel joy. Ironically, having patience is for what is to come, allows you to choose joy now by relaxing into the moment. Not everything will come to us at the exact time that we want it to. Part of cultivating our joy is realizing that everything has its seasons and that sometimes we have a lot of sowing to do before we reap the reward for our labor. We can still find joy through it all.

How to Bring Your Joy Back

When you realize you're giving your power away by focusing on things outside of yourself to bring you joy, you can reclaim it internally. As you become aware of your thoughts that may be robbing you of your joy, you can also become aware of any negative energy or emotions you're holding in your body. If you notice something negative registering in your body, breathe into that space. There may be discomfort or tightness. Just notice whatever is there. See if you can breathe into it. Surround it with love or compassion, just as you would if you knew a friend was feeling the way you do.

It can be helpful to notice how big this space is in your body. Imagine the size and shape of it. Ask yourself what color, texture, or sound this shape might make. Then imagine a powerful stream of light, in whatever color you associate with healing, coming down from the cosmos, straight through your head and into this space. Allow the color to permeate and penetrate the shape; moving in and out and through it. As this healing light surrounds this shape, notice what happens to it. Does it get smaller, lighter, or begin to disappear? Continue to send this light until you feel the shape completely dissolve. This is where you can begin to invite joy back in. See if you can just focus on breathing and tapping into a sense of what it feels like to be alive in your body in this moment. Allow yourself to focus completely on the experience of your own internal energy. Notice sensations in your body: your pulse, your heartbeat. Close your eyes and feel into your heart center. Imagine that it's radiating like a sun, sending peace and joy to all of your cells as they travel throughout your entire being.

I had a friend who used to tell me he would imagine light coming in through the top of his head. He would then direct it into his heart, where it turned all of his cells into a million smiley faces that filled his body with joy and his soul with light. See if this imagery lights you up as well.

Pleasure Exercise

Many of my clients are looking for more joy in their lives. I invite them to begin this investigation by defining what is it that brings them pleasure and writing down everything that comes to mind. This is a free-association exercise, and I ask them to use all of their senses as they create their list.

All kinds of things bring us joy. Some are subtle. For me, it's the smell of coffee roasting in the morning and the first warm sip. It's the large picture window on the north side of the house through which light floods the house each morning as I draw back the blinds. It's the belly laughter of my grandsons as they roll on the rug in a tickling match.

You can also write down the bigger things that give you pleasure. For me, some of those are swimming with giant sea turtles, hearing the roar of the ocean, or walking through a rain forest. Sometimes it is helpful to just focus on each one of your senses separately and see what pleasures comes to mind.

Two wonderful things will be occurring as you write your list. First, your mind, which doesn't know the past from the present, will be experiencing all of the images and memories in real time. As a result, your brain will release endorphins, oxytocin, serotonin, and dopamine. The second benefit is that you're telling your brain that these things are important, and you're sending them along with the endorphins that will help encode them in your memory.

This will enhance your experience of joy and help you to notice more joyful things.

Joyful Giving

In downtown Fort Collins, where I work, there have been many issues with the numbers of homeless people who congregate, panhandle, and sometimes even harass people as they're walking down the street. Having lived in both Los Angeles and Denver, I'd mostly chosen to ignore the panhandlers because I didn't want to engage with anyone who could be a threat to me.

I use a parking lot a couple of blocks from my office, and in the winter, when it gets dark early, I always felt nervous walking to my car because I have to go by a bus stop where several homeless people hang out and I didn't want to be hassled going home.

I've had several friends and family members tell me stories about how they'd made care packages for the homeless or brought them meals. I noticed as they shared these stories, I started to feel uncomfortable inside, as if I wasn't quite aligned with my higher self. As I started to explore this more, I realized what was driving my behavior of ignoring the homeless: it was fear.

Yes, it was OK to be cautious, but I became aware that a great deal of what I feared more than any threat was looking into the eyes of many of these homeless humans. I was afraid of all the pain I might see there. There was something inside of me that felt helpless when I encountered a homeless person and by shutting myself down emotionally, I was trying to protect myself.

It was tough stuff to look at and acknowledge within myself. I realized I wasn't in touch with their suffering because I was afraid of my own. I was afraid of the reality of how these people lived and because of this, I'd discounted our shared humanity.

This was an awakening for me. I'd heard about a millionaire in town who struggled with finding meaning in his life. He drove around with a stack of $50 bills that he'd hand out to the homeless people he encountered. I was told he'd give $50 to people who were alone and $100 to those who had a dog. It gave this gentleman a sense of purpose and joy to see the faces light up as he shared the one thing he had a lot of: money.

Since I'm not a millionaire, I knew this wouldn't be my way to give, but I decided I needed to start being more present with the people who crossed my path. I decided to start greeting homeless people who made eye contact with me, just as I would greet other strangers I would pass on the street. I began connecting with the homeless people I came across with a smile and a simple "Hello" or "Good morning."

The results were amazing. By simply acknowledging the person in front of me, I acknowledged the divine spark that resides within them and that we all share. People responded with big smiles and genuine greetings. There was a moment of shared joy. No matter how different their outer circumstances were, internally, we had a shared humanity—we're all fellow travelers in this journey called life.

One day, as I was walking to my office from my car, a homeless gentleman walked beside me at a quicker pace. He passed me and then turned around briefly as if to say something to me. I noticed that my immediate response was a desire to ignore him due to my still hardwired fight-or-flight response to someone unfamiliar. When we both reached the crosswalk and had to wait for the light, he turned to look at me. I smiled and said, "Good morning." He gave me a huge smile that lit up his face. "Good morning!" he said, "You sure are beautiful!" The light changed, and he walked away, but he left me with a simple gift and a smile—not only on my face, but in my heart.

He didn't want anything from me. When I acknowledged him, he actually had something to give to me. From time to time, homeless people ask me if I can spare any change. But now I feel comfortable looking them in the eye and saying no if I don't have any and giving them a dollar or change when I do. What I notice most often is how people light up for a moment when I greet them with a friendly smile and a few warm words. The gift doesn't have to be monetary. The joy is in just giving of ourselves in whatever ways we can.

There's joy when we give to others, whether it's time, energy, attention, or just sincere words of affirmation. I'm continually amazed at the power of kindness. Just acknowledging someone else can bring moments of shared joy and a feeling of connection to the humanity we share.

I believe that joy is our birthright. It's time to reclaim it and let it manifest in our lives. We can choose to experience more joy no matter what our circumstances are. As we focus on the experience of joy within ourselves, we notice it shows up more frequently in our lives. As we focus on bringing more joy to others, we multiply our own. Joy is an inner spark that shines more brightly when shared. Allow yourself to share your radiant self and see how you light up the world.

Cultivating Joy- Top 5 Takeaways:

1. When you cultivate peace, you make room for joy. Take time to meditate. Drop into your heart, let your thoughts move through you as clouds in the sky, and just breathe.

2. You can actually grow joy! When you experience things that bring you joy, take a few deep breaths and allow yourself to marinate on the good feelings. By focusing on the good feelings, the experience brings, you are telling you mind to notice more things that bring you joy- and it will!

3. Two ways to cultivate joy are to make a list of things that bring you pleasure and plug those things into your calendar, so you experience more of the things that bring you joy, and recall joyful memories. The mind has no concept of time so what you are holding up in your mind is experienced as

now. By recalling a wonderful memory, you are also allowing your now be joyful!

4. Avoid The Waiting Place. You don't have to have everything together, be perfect, or have the perfect circumstances in your life to be in joy. Your true happiness is inside of you. You can choose to be in joy now.

5. You can find joy in giving. As you move out of fear and into love you can practice simple random acts of kindness. When you give your joy to others it is multiplied within you.

Chapter 9

The Future Looks Bright

"The future belongs to those who believe in the beauty of their dreams."

—Eleanor Roosevelt

As you continue to build on your inner resources, you can also enhance your life by looking at what you want to create in it. If you want a life that lights you up, you need to first take inventory of *what* lights up you. Part of doing this is defining what you want to do, be, and have while you still have breath in your body and your feet on this earth.

There are many ways to do this. It can be as simple as making three columns on a piece of paper with the headers "Do," "Be," and "Have" and brainstorming 25 things in each column. This exercise will allow you to define your goals and dreams and help you begin to look at what you really want to create in your life. This list is important because when you don't know what you really want in life, you don't really know what you are moving towards. If you can define what it is you want to do, be, and have in your life, it will help move you forward in the direction of your dreams.

As you begin the "Do" column, you can also refer back to your pleasure exercise. Some of the things you write on this list are things you may have already done and would like to do again. That's OK. This is all about the things you want to do (or keep doing that spark up your life.) This can be, "Go to Europe," "White water river rafting," or "See more sunsets." Allow yourself to create a list that lights you up. Dream big.

In the "Be" column, think of how you'd like to be able to describe yourself to others. You might write, "I am a mountain climber" or "I am an artist." Or, it could be a quality such as, "I am adventurous." If you can't think of 25 things, that's OK. Just write down as many as you can and keep the list handy so that you can add to it later.

The "Have" column can be both material and non-material things you would like to have in your life. There's absolutely nothing wrong with knowing the material things that you'd like to show up in your life. You can also list things such as "serenity" or "more abundance" or "great vacations." Again, let your imagination guide you. The sky's the limit. And as you define what you want to have in your life, you align your mind to help you move toward manifesting it.

What's on Your Bucket List?

There is a great book called *Creating Your Best Life*, written by Caroline Adams Miller and Michael B. Frisch. It's a wonderful guide to defining your goals and developing your bucket list. The authors divide the list into distinctive categories, such as "10 burning desires you have for yourself," "professional and financial goals," and "what if you were given six months to live." All are writing prompts to help you discover what you really want to create and accomplish. By the end of reading the book, you'll have a list of 100 things you want to do before you leave this earth. And there's no time like the present to schedule those things in your calendar to start making those dreams a reality.

Tonight, I dug out that book and looked at the bucket list I'd created nine years ago. I was able to cross 32 things off of the list! It was such an awesome feeling. When we commit to writing down what we truly want in life, it's like putting in a catalog order to the universe. We begin to move toward manifesting those things in our lives.

There's a great journaling exercise to help you figure out what may be on your bucket list. Start by thinking about your childhood. What did you love to do? What kind of dreams did you have for your future? Now, you aren't going to become a superhero, or instantly turn into cowboy, ballerina, or NFL player. But you can begin to get a sense of what lit you up as a child, and you can begin to reintegrate some of those elements into your adult life.

As you remember what thrilled you then, you can see what would enhance your life and bring you joy now. Maybe you were creative and loved to do art. Maybe it was playing soccer or basketball or music. It's never too late to learn. Take those past joys and experience them now by taking a class or joining a local sports team. Go roller-skating or learn how to paint with watercolors. It's amazing how much these activities can enhance your life and bring you a sense of fulfillment.

As a young girl, I spent a lot of time in nature. Between the ages of seven and nine, I lived in Corvallis, Oregon, with my family while my dad was on sabbatical at Oregon State University. Our home was nestled in a lush forest, built on the side of a mountain that couldn't be seen from the road. We had racoons stealing our dog's food from the back deck and deer playing below our tree fort in the back yard. Wild mint grew beside the house, and the smell would settle into our fingers when we picked it. My brother and I would play for hours in those woods, finding salamanders and slugs in the creeks that ran along the property. There was an earthy, dense smell to this forest, which was covered with ferns and flora. It was absolutely magical. I loved the way the sunlight shone through the trees' branches and the feel of the lush green moss that grew on the rocks below. In my happiest, most carefree state, I was very aware of my deep connection to the earth.

I share this with you because when you think of your bucket list, it doesn't have to be grand adventures and walking down the red carpet in Hollywood. By looking back at what was most meaningful to me as a child, I've become aware that one of the things that I want on my bucket list is spending as much time in nature as possible. When I'm in nature, I'm in touch with my soul. So, although there are amazing places I want to visit, and exciting things I want to do on my bucket list, I've also included simple things that deeply light me up as well.

I've taken that love for nature and done wonderful things with it. Three years ago, I climbed to the top of Long's Peak here in Colorado—a journey that began at 3:00 in the morning, with only headlamps to show us the way. In total, it was a 16-hour journey to the summit and back. It took all of my physical and emotional fortitude to reach the top and begin the eight-hour decent back to where my hiking buddy and I had started at the trailhead.

The landscape was breathtaking and diverse throughout the hike. We hiked over boulder fields, walked very narrow pathways on the steep side of the mountain, and had to climb up rocks to get to the summit. But we made it. Hiking Long's Peak was one of the peak experiences of my life, and I'm forever grateful I combined my love of nature with my desire to push myself to the next level and do things I'd never done before. I experienced more beauty than I could have ever imagined and found a deeper sense of myself and my connection to this earth in the process.

I've expanded this love for nature to include hiking, camping, caving, white-water rafting, zip-lining, kayaking, paddle boarding, and scuba diving. These adventures have been some of the greatest experiences of my life.

You can do this too. Remember what lit you up as a kid or in your youth. What lights you up now in adulthood? Often, we get so busy and caught up with our careers, or raising children, or trying to make ends meet that we forget that life is more than just survival. We can infuse it with more meaning if we pause and take inventory of what holds meaning for us. Then, we can integrate it to create a bright and fulfilling existence in which we feel fully alive.

A bucket list doesn't have to be only things you haven't done before. It can be remembering to do the things that have been meaningful for you in the past that you'd like to reintegrate into your life now. As you make these things more of a priority, they'll bring you more joy and allow you to expand in new and greater ways. This is a wonderful way you can remember your roots while still reaching for the stars. A brighter future awaits you.

What Makes You Shine

Dr. Lynn Owens has worked in academia for almost 40 years. She's a dynamic and brilliant woman who has dedicated her life to helping people identify and focus on their strengths and showing them how to achieve their highest level of performance.

Lynn worked at the University of Maryland for 18 years and at Montana State University for 16 years, which is where she developed a class called "The Ethic of Care." This class helped students get in touch with not only *who* they were, but *how* they were in the world. By using a remarkable tool called the ProScan Survey, which has 30 years of research behind it and a 96 percent reliability rate, Lynn has been able to help students identify what their strengths are, how stress affects them, and most importantly, how to maximize their performance in all areas of their lives.

Lynn's class helps encourage students to foster better relationships with themselves and others, as well as to harness the strengths of their personality. Class projects involved developing a caring friendship with someone outside of the class to understand the dynamics of what constitutes good relationships.

When I interviewed Lynn for *The Spark*, she discussed her own journey and how she went from being a rather lost 19-year-old who was about to be kicked out of college to an extremely successful, motivated, professional who has continued to find her voice, identify her calling, and share her tremendous gifts with others.

Through her amazing ability to connect with her students and ProScan, thousands of people have achieved their goals by being aware of their greater gifts, taking better care of themselves, and discovering their true calling. Lynn helps others focus on what's right with them (rather than what's wrong with them) and how to become the best versions of themselves. Her contribution in helping others create bigger and brighter futures for themselves is astounding.

You don't have to use the ProScan to find out what makes you shine or how you want to light up your future. Spend some time reflecting and journal about what truly brings meaning to your life. I saw a presenter that goes by the name of Nuirka in the fall of 2018 in Los Angeles. In her early career she was a trainer for Tony Robbins, and for the last 20 years has been writing books and giving workshops all over the world to help people create their best lives. She had a wealth of wisdom and knowledge to share and was a truly inspirational speaker. My biggest take away from the event was what she shared about the importance of asking ourselves high-quality questions each day. Nuirka said when we wake up in the morning and our self-questions are, "Why do I have to go to work today?" or "What will go wrong today?" we are setting ourselves up for negative answers and so we go about our day with low vibrational and low emotional energy. When we ask ourselves high quality questions, we give ourselves higher quality answers. "What if today was one of the best days of my life?" "How would I feel if I felt I really gave my best at work today?" "How can I best serve those I come into contact with?" These are questions that result in a higher level of consciousness and more positive emotional experience. You can create a brighter future by asking yourself higher quality questions now and then follow the answers and watch them bloom in your life.

Luminous Life

After interviewing Dr. Jacob Liberman on *The Spark*, I remember walking out of the studio and saying to my producer, "I have no idea what just happened." The interview felt timeless, and I felt a deep sense of connection to Jacob and his message. Time had taken on a new dimension, and I felt a heightened state of awareness just through our conversation. Jacob is a world-renowned doctor, scientist, and international presenter, who has helped thousands of people change their lives, get liberated from physical and emotional ailments, and heal themselves.

Jacob initially wanted to go to school to become a dentist, but after a series of serendipitous events, he ended up going to optometry school, which changed his life in amazing ways.

"Seeing is the most important thing in our lives," he said. "Both outer seeing and internal seeing." He spoke about how our physicality is designed to initiate action and how everything we do is a response to something that catches our eye. Internally, our inner eye of awareness grabs us and suddenly moves us in a certain direction, which is what we call "inspiration." And that inspiration breathes life into us.

Jacob discussed the ways in which we can build resilience by letting go of our preconceived notions of how life "has to be." He said that we have to quiet the constant chatter in our minds, tune in to our inner GPS, and trust that our internal guidance system will lead us into our best lives.

What I learned from him is that the more we quit striving for perfection and seeking external happiness, the more we can relax into an inner knowingness that allows us to become successful at living. When we approach life from this mindset, our inner angst and stress are reduced tremendously.

Before I interviewed him, I read his book *Luminous Life*— twice. I wanted to memorize as much of the important information he shared as I possibly could. Because of a profound incident 40 years ago in which his own eyesight was improved by 300 percent, Jacob set out on a lifelong journey through quantum physics and neuroscience so that he could help replicate his results with others. His goal was to help them heal not only their eyesight, but their hearts as well.

The statement that had the biggest impact on me was "Life is looking for you!" I love this. If life is looking for us, we can let go of all the desperate clinging to things and searching outside of us for something that will create happiness. If life is looking for us and we trust it to show up for us, we can relax into the knowledge that life will continue to provide us with the lessons, opportunities, and experiences we need to continue to grow and evolve into all we've hoped and dreamed we'd become. We can trust that life itself will illuminate our way.

Now, this doesn't mean we shouldn't plan, dream, or have goals. Those are all wonderful, important things. We can do all of that and trust that life (divine guidance) will illuminate our path. When we come from this more relaxed place in our relationship with life, we're able to navigate life's inevitable rough waters more easily. We develop a depth of resilience that allows us to handle the conflicts and challenges with more ease and grace, trusting that our internal GPS is always working for us.

It reminds me of a little framed card I had beside my bed for years, which read, "All of the strength, beauty, and happiness you are searching for is right there inside of you." Jacob's words and life exemplify a deeper, spiritual way to access resilience and grit. It's through trusting life itself. Believing that the same power that aligns the planets, beats in our hearts, and changes the seasons will guide us into our best lives.

As fate would have it, I was gifted a trip to Maui with my daughter Hailey in August of 2018. We had an amazing time being on the beach of Kapalua Bay, snorkeling with giant sea turtles, and sailing alongside a pod of more than a hundred spinner dolphins. Everything dream vacations are made of. The only thing that made it even more special was that I was able to spend time with Jacob and share two mornings with him.

Once again, my time with Jacob took on a timeless dimension. I felt a deep connection with him and complete comfort in his presence. My daughter joined us for breakfast the second day and not only immediately loved

Jacob, but she was absolutely thrilled because actor Owen Wilson (who lives on the island) happened to be eating at the table right beside us. Talk about feeling lit up!

Jacob discussed the importance of following your heart when you're inspired to do something, at the moment it's sparked—for example, making a phone call when a certain person comes to mind and you feel the urge to reach out. It's trusting that those impulses show up for a reason and that they're life guiding us on our path.

This happens in the same way that a bear gets signals from the environment that the weather is changing. Jacob explained, "The bear doesn't have to consciously think, 'Wow, it's getting colder. I should probably go to Target and buy a coat!' The bear just follows its natural guidance and begins to grow a thicker coat of fur for the winter." That same guidance is always available to us if we're present to its natural unfolding in our lives.

These are powerful messages that can help us relax and trust that the guiding presence within us is always bringing us to our highest good.

A Guiding Light

Part of creating a spark-filled life is to realize that the sparks are already alive within us. We aren't separate from the spark. We *are* the spark. When I've trusted this inner guidance, it's led me to exactly where I needed to be—and to do exactly what I needed to do—at important times in my life.

One great example of this was in 1991, when I was a single mother living in downtown Denver. I had a daily commute of 45 minutes to drop my three-year-old daughter, Acacia, off at day care, and then make it to work at The Care Unit of Colorado, where I worked as a mental health counselor on the adolescent unit.

I'd been working on the adolescent unit for a year and a half, and I'd had the privilege of being the only person on the therapy staff without a master's degree. I loved the adolescents I worked with and had a deep connection with the three female staff members with whom I worked closely.

On January 14, a date I'll never forget, 12 friends of mine from Denver and Fort Collins were all at my aunt's home in Eagle/Vail. My many friends had filled the beautiful house, nestled among aspen trees on the ninth hole of the golf course, with laughter and merriment. We had an awesome time skiing, sledding, dining, and drinking together. But on the last night, as I was getting ready to go to bed, I suddenly felt overwhelmed with emotion. "What's wrong?" my friend Elle asked. "I don't know," I said with tears in my eyes. "I am just getting the strongest hit that I need to move back to Fort Collins."

She looked at me quizzically, "You have such great friends in Denver. You have an awesome career. Why in the world would you want to move back there?" I couldn't give her an answer. All that I knew was that something deep inside of me was guiding me to go home to Fort Collins.

I called my mom the next day and told her of my strong feelings and my conviction that I needed to move back home. She told me that ironically, the gentleman who had been renting the basement of their rental home, had given notice and would be out by February 1. If I wanted the apartment, it was mine. My lease in Denver was going to be up on February 1 as well, so it was perfect timing. I immediately said that I'd take it. When I got back to Denver, that Monday, I gave my two weeks' notice at work. Two weeks later, I'd packed up and moved back home.

Within a few days after moving back to Fort Collins, I had a new job, and my daughter and I began to settle into a new life. And then, it happened. Three weeks to the day, after I'd moved back to Fort Collins, the adolescent unit where I'd worked was on the front page of the *Rocky Mountain News* with the headline "Psychiatric Abuses Charged." The unit where I had worked with my very dear friends had been shut down, all of my girlfriends had been laid off, and the adolescent unit was permanently shut down in that hospital.

Apparently, unbeknownst to any of us, the unit had had scouts traveling around the nation to find adolescents who had insurance that would pay for extended stays. Because this was in the days before managed care, we had adolescents on the unit anywhere from three to nine months until their insurance ran out. These scouts were receiving a $5,000 kickback per kid who entered the unit.

If I hadn't followed my inner guidance, I would have been a single mom without a job and no way to support my daughter and me. I would have signed another lease February 1, and I would not have been able to afford it. I don't know what I would have done. I don't know how I would have survived. By listening to my inner guidance, I was able to continue to flourish and provide for our needs.

We all have this inner guidance. You can create a bright future through stillness, awareness, and being open to that light within you. When you follow your inner GPS you can allow it to illuminate your way to the spark-filled life that awaits.

The Future Looks Bright – Top 5 Takeaways

1. Write out a list of 25 things you want to do, be, and have. By defining what you want in your life you have a greater chance of getting it, experiencing it, and creating it in your life.
2. Create your bucket list. You can use helpful resources to help you define your list like in the book, *Creating Your Best Life*. You can also add to your bucket list by journaling about what you loved as a child and the dreams you had for yourself that you still would like to manifest in the future.
3. You can enhance your future as you find your personal strengths. You can use tools like the ProScan or other strength finders to help you see the areas you excel in so you can build upon those and find greater opportunities to do what lights you up.

4. Ask yourself quality questions to help enhance your life. "How do I show up as my best self?" or "What would make today really great?" are great questions that prime your brain to focus on seeking and seeing those answers manifest in your life.

5. Life is looking for you. When you trust your higher power and your internal guidance system it will guide you to a bright and wonderful future. Your inner guidance is available at all times. By quieting your mind and tuning in, it will lead you to the life you truly desire.

Chapter 10

Contribution

"Only those who have learned the power of sincere and selfless contribution experience life's deepest joy: true fulfillment."

—Tony Robbins

When I think of what fully illuminates our lives, it's the ability to contribute something good to the world. When I think of the word "contribution," there's no bigger or better example of this than my own mother. It's been her life story, her journey, which has so deeply impacted my own.

Growing up on a sugar beet and dairy farm, my mother, born Judy Land, was raised in near poverty. Her clothes were handsewn, she had few toys, but her heart was full, and she always felt blessed. When I was a little girl, she would tell me stories of her youth and the amazing star-filled sky she would gaze at while she sat out in the pastures on her beloved donkey, Amigo, until bedtime.

My mother was raised as a very hard worker, and she learned that in order to survive, people had to contribute to the greater good. But my mother's giving went beyond that. I know a large part of this "gift to give" came from her mother, my grandmother Dorthey.

When my mother was a little girl, she sometimes felt embarrassed by my grandmother's ability to stop and connect with everyone she met. Dorthey never knew a stranger. Heck, she even made birthday cakes for them. Seriously. If my grandmother met you and she knew it was your birthday, she'd whip you up one of the most beautiful celebratory desserts you've ever seen. She was a master cake decorator.

On the farm, they often hired migrant workers, who were even more impoverished than my mother's family, and they would give them free housing in a little home they had on their property. My grandmother was an amazing cook, and there was always room at her table for just a few more. No one went hungry around her. She and my grandfather didn't have money, but they had meat and eggs. And they shared them with whomever needed food in their small community.

My mother talks about how her mother loved and accepted everyone. She was also very strong and not afraid to confront people whom she felt were hurting either her or other people's feelings. She was always caring and standing up for other people who couldn't stand up for themselves.

Grandma Dorthey taught Sunday school and always brought food for the weekly dinners at church. She contributed through what she had to give: her time, attention, and culinary talents. If anyone in the community was ill, she'd bring them a home-cooked meal, company, and conversation.

Unafraid of people's misery, she was an amazing listener, and she took the time to connect with others at a heart level. When she became an Avon representative after all of her children had left the farm, she didn't make a lot of money at first because she always brought a coffee cake to each of the homes she'd visit. She probably spent more money on the ingredients for the cakes than she ever took home in sales—a true testament to the joy she had in giving.

When my grandmother died at 63, robbed of life by cancer, the little white church in Timnath, Colorado, was overflowing at her funeral. Past the point of standing room only in the back, the crowd that had come with thankful hearts to pay respect to this outstanding woman spilled onto the front yard.

After her death, a stained-glass window was made for that church to honor her life. It depicts Noah's ark, the rainbow, and the dove with the olive branch in its beak. Every time I revisit that little church, I look at the light reflecting through it, and I think of the light that my grandmother reflected throughout her life. I think of a courageous woman who included everyone with whom she came into contact and the many, many people she saved from "drowning" as she gathered them "two by two" and took care of them. What an amazing woman.

This was the example my mother grew up with. And so, she too became a giver, an includer, and a contributor. It was in her DNA. As I was growing up, my mother was always on the PTA. She room mother for both my brother and me at school. And she involved herself in each and every activity we were involved in. Let me tell you, there were a lot!

My mother was my Girl Scout leader, my 4-H cooking instructor, and the one who fixed my 4-H sewing projects, which I could never get quite right. When I won the science fair in sixth grade, I'm pretty sure she won it for me, given all the time and effort she put into helping me complete my project.

Our birthday parties were the best. Each one had a theme and was attended by all the friends we could muster up. Like my grandmother, my mother always said, "the more the merrier," and that meant we had a whole lot of "merry" going on at our house for all of these celebrations.

Mom made each holiday special. Not only would she help us make decorations for every occasion on the calendar, but she'd decorate the house, make it magical for every season, and fill our tummies with the seasonal recipes she'd learned from her mother. It was a magical childhood with her at the helm. Until it all came crashing down.

I honestly don't know how she survived it. After 18 years with a man she adored, her marriage and the life she loved dissolved in front of her. She could only stand on the sidelines and watch the flood (my father) erase from her life everything she knew and held most important: her family.

This was tragic. But her story is one of contribution—not collapse. My mother went to hell and back. But after a year of deep despair, she arose like the phoenix from the ashes and regained her life. Not only did she survive—she thrived.

For 33 years she owned Paul Wood Florist, and there she kept a working crew that became her second family. People weren't just employed by Judy. They were adopted by her. For 21 years she taught floral design at Colorado State University. To this day, she teaches a class at Front Range Community College. She loves her students. Over the years, she's told me about the painful stories her students have shared with her and her efforts to help them. She'd stay long after class to lend a loving ear for whatever they were going through.

In 1994, my mother got involved in the Rotary Club— "a global network of 1.2 million neighbors, friends, leaders, and problem-solvers who see a world where people unite and take action to create lasting change—across the globe, in our communities, and in ourselves." In 2004, she was the president of the local chapter in Fort Collins. And in 2015, she was named "Rotarian of the Year" for all of the hard work, effort, and service she's provided to that organization along with many, many people in our community and beyond.

Most days, if I'm walking around Old Town, where my mother's shop stood for 33 years, I feel as though I can't avoid running into someone who knows her, who then tells me how wonderful she is or how she's helped them in some way. It's something that I've grown used to and never tire of hearing.

She's been my cheerleader, my best friend, and my safety net when I've fallen and needed her to catch me in her loving arms. She's given innumerable hours to me, my daughters, my grandsons, my siblings, and many others, without any expectation of anything in return. Her joy has always been in bringing joy to others.

My mother has been a constant model of what it means to be selfless. Whenever I felt down about something, she'd say, "Well, you just need to go volunteer somewhere, and you will feel better!" She knew the value of contribution. As we give, we receive. As we help others grow and improve their lives, our inner life grows as well. I'm so deeply grateful for the powerful role model she's been in helping me understand this powerful gift of giving.

The Best Version of Ourselves

I've adapted a prosperity mindset exercise I learned from Weldon Long. In addition to using it myself every day, I use it with my clients, my friends, and my family members. It's a great tool for getting rid of limiting beliefs and instilling the beliefs necessary to create the best life possible. In this exercise, you write down the negative thoughts or limiting beliefs that are holding you back and then write out the beliefs you would like to believe about yourself instead (even if you don't fully believe them now.) Examples of negative or limiting beliefs are,

"I always struggle with money."

"There are no good men (or women) left to date."

"My body looks terrible."

"I'm unlucky."

These are the kind of beliefs that are the habitual, and often subconscious, thoughts we repeat in our heads all day long. Dig into what your beliefs are in the areas of finances, relationships, career, health and fitness, spirituality, and self-concept and see what comes to mind. If it is a negative belief, it doesn't necessarily mean that it is true; you have just been repeating it over and over in your head for so long it *feels* true. Reaching for the thoughts you would like to believe about yourself instead are the first steps to correcting this.

After you have written all that down, imagine you are a year into the future and all of those new beliefs you wrote down have come true. Feel into that place and imagine what that would truly be like to have instilled those new positive beliefs in your mind. From that place, you will begin the actual document you will read out loud to yourself each day. Begin by writing out a gratitude statement utilizing the image you just had and write it down in positive present tense language. For example:

"I am so grateful and thankful I have abundant wealth."

"I am thankful for my loving relationship and for all the joy I experience each day."

"I feel so blessed to have a career that I love, and I am excited to go to work each morning."

Then, for the second part, focus on writing affirmations, such as "I am" statements. Under each one, write out a couple of simple, but specific action steps you will take to make that statement true. For example, if the affirmation is "I am healthy and physically fit," the action steps would be:

1. I work out 20 minutes a day, 3 times per week.

2. I make nutritious food choices."

The more specifically written they are, the better. This process helps to carve new neuropathways in your mind and change long-standing, habitual thoughts into an improved self-concept, which will enable you to create a better version of yourself.

What is also great about this process is that it can really reinforce new positive behaviors in your life. When you read the affirmation in the example above, that you are make good food choices and start to reach for a doughnut instead you will actually experience something called cognitive dissonance in your mind. Because you have been affirming that you make good food choices day after day, something internally doesn't feel right which signals the brain to say, "Hey! Something isn't right here!" Often it is just this pause that allows you to stop and make the right choice that aligns with your daily affirmations.

The final part of the exercise, which follows gratitude, affirmation and the action plan, is on contribution. It can also be the most powerful. Imagine again that everything you have written down so far has come true. Then imagining you have become the person you have envisioned; how would you be better able to contribute to the world?" Write this down in present tense language, as well. A few examples are:

"I am so thankful I get to contribute so much joy and kindness to the world."

"Now that I am so financially abundant, I can contribute to the charities of my choice."

"My gifts help others heal and see the light within themselves, and they help them shine and share their own light with the rest of the world."

"I chose to smile and greet all those who come across my path and spread the seeds of kindness."

It doesn't have to be something monetary. It can be giving of yourself as a volunteer, or just making the choice to contribute more love to the world by your own interactions with it.

I read my mindset aloud to myself every morning and I encourage you to do the same. By reading your mindset out loud, you're speaking these things into your life. It is such an important thing to do this and to train your thoughts and behaviors in this way. As you allow yourself to heal, you're able to share that healing with your friends, your family members, your communities, and this world. Your personal healing actually becomes your greatest contribution to others. We are not victims of this world. We can empower ourselves to make substantial change by focusing on hanging our own negative beliefs and behaviors. As we do this, our interactions with others improve, we are kinder and more empathetic, and this energy becomes a healing balm for ourselves and humanity. How we feel and what we do matters and contributes to the collective whole.

Being a Great Contributor

My interview with Curt Richardson, the CEO, Chief Visionary Officer, and creator and founder of OtterBox, was truly inspirational. His personal journey into entrepreneurialism started in his youth, and by seventh grade, he'd launched his first business, Curt's Lawn Service. He hasn't stopped since.

Curt is an amazingly successful individual. But perhaps what impressed me the most about him was his deep, heartfelt drive to give back. The mission statement at OtterBox is "We Grow to Give" and this is apparent through the many foundations Curt and his wife, Nancy, have developed, which make an impact at the community level and far beyond.

In 2010, they began the OtterCares Foundation, which educates and inspires youth to become entrepreneurs and philanthropists. Not only does the program grow confidence, build character, and enhance leadership skills in these future business creators, but it teaches these children that when they give of their time, talent, or treasure, their hearts grow fuller, and this forms the habit of lifelong giving.

Also, one day a year, OtterBox shuts business down worldwide and turns it into a volunteer day for their 1,200 employees. Aside from the way it benefits the community, OtterBox employees say that this day of giving ignites sparks in them to continue to help others and that it enhances their own lives.

Blue Ocean Foundation is a nonprofit that Curt and Nancy created to "be a catalyst in our community through impactful giving that supports economic growth." The foundation also puts up all of the lights in Old Town Fort Collins during the winter months, which transforms the whole area into a magical place. I told Curt that the lights affect me personally because I work in Old Town and they lift my spirits each year. The foundation also provides the fireworks on the Fourth of July, which brings the community together in an important and wonderful way.

Curt and Nancy's personal foundation, the Richardson Foundation, gives away a percentage of the profits from the company that goes directly into this foundation. In September 2017, hurricanes Irma and Maria hit the British Islands, where Curt and Nancy have one of their homes. Seventy percent of the homes' roofs were gone after the hurricanes, and there was extensive damage and destruction to the islands. Through Curt and Nancy's donations and work with the Convoy of Hope, a huge ship came to the islands with food, fuel, and water and fed the territory for three months. The Richardson Foundation continues to help rebuild the communities of these beautiful islands.

"It was a blessing to be able to do that," Curt told me. When I asked him what he felt his greatest lesson in business had been, he said, "To be the best steward of what you've been given, share it, and give it back."

In the end, we can't take it all with us. As my father used to say, there is no U-Haul that follows us to the gravesite. When we give our talents and our time—contributing to others by just having listening ears, helping hands, and an open heart—we're gifting the world in powerful ways. Each act of our giving goes out in concentric circles that returns to our hearts tenfold in the process. Through his life and business experiences, Curt Richardson is a true example of that.

The Gift of Our Stories

For almost 30 years, I've sat and listened to people tell me the stories of their lives. These are powerful testaments to the resilience we have within us and our ability to survive our circumstances. There's power in our stories. I'm often aware that I may be the only one with whom these amazing people share the deepest contents of their hearts. Although I feel honored and privileged to be in this place of trust in so many people's lives, I also realize how many others could gain strength and courage from hearing those stories. And your story.

We've all experienced people who are negative and who just want to complain about their woes. Interacting with them while they dump all their difficulties can feel like a huge burden. That's not the kind of storytelling I'm talking about. It's telling your story from a place of having taken your inner inventory and gleaned wisdom from your experiences. It's being able to share your authentic self. Your light helps illuminate others.

When we share our stories of struggle, suffering, triumph, and courage, we give other people the gift of being able to be in touch with their own humanity. We help them have hope, gain strength, and heal. This is why doing our own healing work is so essential. It's the biggest gift we can give the world. Healing our past, owning our story, and sharing it with others is an amazing way to contribute to concentric rings of healing that can extend far beyond ourselves.

Inspirational author Alexandra Elle writes, "You're not a victim for sharing your story. You are a survivor setting the world on fire with your truth. And you never know who needs your light, your warmth, and raging courage."

Find ways to share your story with others. Take inventory of the gifts you've been given, the lessons you've learned, and the ways you've experienced joy, defeat, connection, fortitude, sorrow, and delight. Share those in whatever way feels appropriate. Our shared humanity yearns for connection, acceptance, and acknowledgment. When we can move out of our egos (which tell us to always look good and as though we have it all together), we give others permission to be themselves more fully and to be more fully human.

Get in touch with your inner light. As you become aware of your gifts, abilities, and talents, you can begin to share them with people around you—coworkers, friends, or family members. This is actually one of the most selfless things you can do. Healing yourself and getting in touch with what creates joy, sparks, and light in your life *is* your contribution to the world and helps illuminate us all.

Random Acts of Kindness

Last January, I began a Random Acts of Kindness women's group. This is a group of nine powerful women who gather once a month to show up authentically and be present for one another as we work on self-growth and contribution.

One of the ways this group contributes to a bigger cause is through donation. Each woman brings $20 to the meeting, and whoever is facilitating the group that month chooses a charity or cause to which we donate the money. One month, it was to a father who had just been widowed and was facing the daunting task of raising two little boys alone. One month, it was to a nonprofit to raise safety awareness. Even though it may not seem like a large amount of money, it feels wonderful to give in that way.

The women in this group also contribute by making food to share and creating the space to speak and listen to one another with open hearts. Each woman contributes to the conversation and the magic that is created there when we hold each other's hearts in reverence. Through deep listening and caring about one another, we help to heal each another and more deeply grow ourselves. This group becomes like the pebble in the pond and from this meeting, each one of us enters back into the world with more to share and contribute. And the concentric circles continue.

We contribute to the world when we give of ourselves and engage in random acts of kindness with one other. Our contribution doesn't have to be monetary. The simplest act of kindness has a ripple effect. Allowing a car to go in front of us in traffic, opening a door for someone, a smile or a greeting to a stranger—each one of these acts are important. We never know how we might be showing up as an angel in somebody else's life. There's no greater feeling than to know that we've added value and improved someone's life in some way.

One day, I was having a rough morning, and I was in the drive-through line at Starbucks. When I got to the window to pay, the gentleman at the counter said, "There is no charge. The person in front of you paid for your meal." I smiled ear to ear! This small random act of kindness changed my whole day. It reminded me that there really are more loving people in the world than we may realize.

Be one of those people.

This is a time in our world's history in which we need to focus on contributing to the greater good. We have a political climate that diversifies and divides us. We need to be aware of how we are contributing positively to our planet and be aware of how we are impacting it. Through our conscious daily acts, we put into motion the ripple effects that can help heal the world. These ripple back to us, healing us as well. Our contributions, big or small, are this transformative power.

Contribution- Top 5 Takeaways

1. Think who has role modeled giving and contribution in your life. What did you learn from them? How could you emulate their actions or give in your own way?

2. We can break through our own limiting beliefs about ourselves and our world and move to gratitude, affirmation and action, and then to contribution. Write down your positive mindset and watch these areas grow in your in your life.

3. Share your story and your gifts with others. You have wisdom inside of you. You may just be the angel that someone else in needing in their life right now. As you shine your light on others, you help to ignite the sparks within them as well.

4. Consider joining a group that has a component of contribution and giving. There is collective power in these groups and everyone's energy and gifts contribute to the whole. If there isn't a group like the Random Acts of Kindness group in your area, consider beginning one of your own. Even if you start with just 3 or 4 people, collective minds make a difference and our collective hearts can change the world.

5. Think about ways you can contribute to your community, your family or friends, or even to total strangers. Gifting others, even anonymously, helps to spread positivity and will light you up inside as well.

Chapter 11

Igniting the Spark

"Inside of us is a place that is all-knowing, all mighty,

which is a fragment of God.

There is a spark inside each one of us."

- Wayne Dyer

As I write this last chapter, I want you to know that this is not the end. It's only the beginning. The beginning of you taking your life to a new level—of allowing your sparks to ignite and illuminate your life and the lives of those around you.

It only takes a moment to pause, put your palms together, and feel the energy surging between them. If you focus on this, you can feel the sensation expanding. You can feel the aliveness. This is your spark. If you want to create a spark-filled life, you have to allow this inner spark to emerge, to ignite, and to become a full flame. That requires focusing on what you want to create in your life, letting go of the past, and living full force in the present moment.

This means allowing yourself to define who you are and who you want to become, transcending circumstances and limiting beliefs to become the greatest version of yourself. This is how you create the inner strength and resilience to not only be present to this world but contribute to it in a profound way.

An amazing power lies within us. It's been called by many names: higher self, holy spirit, the universe, God, and pure essence. It's the part of us that can't be burned, drowned, or blown away. It's the part of us that knows our potential and yearns for us to grow into our greatest self. No matter what you call it, most of us are aware of something greater than ourselves. When we're in touch with this inner power, miracles begin to show up in our lives.

You have this light within you. You have this spark. You were born with it. Even if it's gotten covered up with life's challenging circumstances, false beliefs, grief, and behavior that doesn't serve you, your essence is still glowing in there. You can excavate it. You can add positive fuel and ignite it. You can change your life through your desire and intention. Nurturing the spark within you is the key to creating a life that is full of joy, peace, resilience, and connectedness.

We're at a crucial moment in our world. It's imperative that we do the deeper inner work to bring out the best version of ourselves so that we can be agents of positive change on this planet. Can you imagine what we could do if each one of us brought as much love and healing to the world as possible?

We have this power within us to make a difference. Our collective co-hearts can change the world.

Your own healing is actually your biggest contribution to the rest of humanity. You can change your thoughts, the way you feel, and the way you act and respond to others. This creates a ripple effect that brings love and healing to everyone you meet. We are all important threads in this tapestry called life. Together, we can make create a beautiful world for ourselves and for each other.

It begins with you. You can do it. You can create a spark-filled life that makes your goals, dreams, and visions a reality. You can. You can.

The world is waiting for you.

Special Thanks

This book would not have been possible without the help of many, many amazing friends and family who loved and supported me, and continued to be my greatest cheerleaders as I wrote this book.

Deepest Gratitude:
To my loving Mom and Pops (my original fan club) for your unconditional love and support and for being amazing sounding boards. I love you both a million apple pies! I know, "I got the best ones"!

To my brother for being one of my very best friends (You got any gum?). You inspire me to be my best self through your own example and make me laugh till my sides hurt every time we're together.

To my dearest friends and soul sisters Shelly, Cindy, and Jenny, whom make me feel connected, grounded, and loved each and every day in this world. I am blessed beyond measure to have you in my life.

To my soul tribe members Kip and Stevey for all of their hard and patient work with me in all the technical areas where I am not so hot and for being two people I can always rely on. I love you both.

To my copyeditor Lauren Brombert for all of her extra hours of work and helping me to expand my ideas.

To my dear friends, mentors, and inspirations Misa and Jacob for their love and light. Thank you for believing in me and helping me to see the spark in myself.

To my daughters and grandsons who I love with all of my heart and are my favorite, funniest, and largest lights in my world.

And finally, to my producer Chris Lanphear, for all of his love, support, extreme patience, and passion for what we continue to create together for The Spark and for asking the fateful question that day, "Have you ever thought of doing your own radio show?" You have changed my life and I am forever grateful.

About Stephanie James

Stephanie James is a psychotherapist, dynamic public speaker, and published author with nearly 30 years of experience in the mental health field. Nominated for Fort Collins Woman of The Year in 2014 and a graduate of Colorado State University and the University of Denver, Stephanie has an unrelenting commitment to help others achieve their best lives and to become the best versions of themselves.

Stephanie has been leading workshops in the Rocky Mountain region since 2007 and is the creative visionary and host of The Spark Summit, a gathering of today's thought leaders in the areas of psychology, spirituality, and science, designed to help people break through limiting beliefs and behaviors and live their best lives.

Her weekly radio show and podcast The Spark with Stephanie James is a show designed to inspire, motivate and help others to ignite their very best lives. Produced by Chris Lanphear and Noco.fm, The Spark features experts in their fields, as well as the everyday heroes who make our world a better place just by being in it.

Stephanie has a passion for connecting with people from all walks of life. Her mission is to bring as much love and healing to the world as possible. She is a leader in a local Random Acts of Kindness women's group and she spends her free time with her beloved dog Jewels, her two beautiful daughters, and jumping on the trampoline with her grandsons.

Made in the USA
Monee, IL
04 November 2020